ONE TREE AT A TIME

ONE TREE AT A TIME

Thriving in the face of adversity...

FELICITY EAGAN

BALBOA.
PRESS

A DIVISION OF HAY HOUSE

Unless otherwise noted all **Scripture taken from the New King James Version**®. **Copyright © 1982 by Thomas Nelson. Used by permission.**

References: [1] –Thompson, Bert Ph.D. - Apologetics Press – *"Biblical Accuracy and Circumcision on the 8th Day"* http://www.apologeticspress.org/apcontent.aspx?category=13&article=1118

References: The words at [2] and [3] –were first read in the book by -Shah, Hannah. – (Rider – Ebury Publishing, 2010) – *"The Imam's Daughter"*. It was an extract from a beautiful and moving poem called *"The Invitation"* –by Oriah © Mountain Dreaming, which can also be found in her book *"The Invitation"* -(HarperONE, Sanfrancisco, 1999) or at www.oriahmountaindreamer.com

Balboa Press books may be ordered through booksellers or by contacting:

Balboa Press
A Division of Hay House
1663 Liberty Drive
Bloomington, IN 47403
www.balboapress.com.au
1 (877) 407-4847

Because of the dynamic nature of the Internet, any web addresses or links contained in this book may have changed since publication and may no longer be valid. The views expressed in this work are solely those of the author and do not necessarily reflect the views of the publisher, and the publisher hereby disclaims any responsibility for them.

The author of this book does not dispense medical advice or prescribe the use of any technique as a form of treatment for physical, emotional, or medical problems without the advice of a physician, either directly or indirectly. The intent of the author is only to offer information of a general nature to help you in your quest for emotional and spiritual well-being. In the event you use any of the information in this book for yourself, which is your constitutional right, the author and the publisher assume no responsibility for your actions.

Any people depicted in stock imagery provided by Thinkstock are models, and such images are being used for illustrative purposes only.
Certain stock imagery © Thinkstock.

Printed in the United States of America.

ISBN: 978-1-4525-2654-6 (sc)
ISBN: 978-1-4525-2655-3 (e)

Balboa Press rev. date: 11/12/2014

"To those God has used to support, encourage, teach and challenge me..."

Contents

Foreword

I have known Felicity Eagan for over 20 years and have watched as she struggled to establish her relationship with God. It has been my pleasure to walk with her through many sorrows, hurts, anxieties and life changing experiences until at last she has discovered the inexpressible beauty of God's grace.

Over the last few years God has stripped away everything that she holds dear, challenging Felicity to consider a path that, in her wildest dreams, she would never have wanted. As she has come to terms with her intended path, I have witnessed the fear and anxiety of the past be replaced with strength and an indescribable inner beauty.

This book has been born out of an overwhelming passion to encourage other women who may be going through similar situations. Her heart's desire is that others learn from and identify with her experiences. As you read these devotions you will get a sense of the raw honesty that each one shares. They will make you laugh, they may cause you to cry, and they will challenge and inspire you to greatness. Most have been written after a learning experience and many are based on real life events. In the pages of this book you will find a kindred spirit that is just like you, doing the journey, warts and all, loving Jesus and allowing Him to be her guide.

My prayer is that you will find comfort, joy and freedom as you take the time to meditate on these words and as Felicity opens her heart to you, through the pages of this book, that you will be inspired to discover your destiny and find the courage to fulfill it.

Felicity has a call on her life to be a missionary and the sales from this book will go towards supporting her through her theological training and once on the field.

Your support is greatly appreciated.
Paula

Preface

Never in my wildest dreams did I ever imagine I would be a published author... then again, never in my wildest dreams did I think I would stand up willing to be counted as one who would serve as an inter-cultural missionary or have a heart for 'women's ministry'. Yet here I am doing all three and it is only by the grace of God that it is possible at all.

In fact, it wasn't that long ago that I stood at a crossroad where I was dangerously drawn towards death and its lure consumed my every waking hour. I irrationally craved it and the solace that I thought it would bring. I was jaded, I was tired and I was overwhelmed by life's relentless struggles.

But I have learnt that *"God delivers those drawn towards death"* and by His grace He miraculously delivered me from a 'spirit of heaviness'. There was no wild exorcism in fact the exact opposite was true. I was on my own in my dark hallway and His voice to my heart brought release. *"You need to bind the spirit of heaviness"*... that was all it took and I physically felt a burden lift from my shoulders and from that point onward the desire to take my own life left me. He replaced the grieving of my soul with an inexpressible joy and gave me a will to live beyond and above the circumstances of my life.

This devotional can be traced back to my bath tub where I laid soaking only a few months after this experience. Perhaps my nakedness at that time was a preface of what God was about to ask of me but nevertheless the irony of my 'raw state' was not wasted and brings a smile to my face even now. I wanted to give something back. God had saved my life both physically and spiritually and I wanted this new life He had given me to count for something, to bring glory to Him. So as I laid there dreamily, I started thinking that there must be other women like me in my church who would turn up at church on Sunday with their 'happy faces' on only to fall apart as soon as they got home.

Surely there were other women who wanted 'real' relationships with God and with others and fellowship that operated outside the realms of 'holier than thou' expectations and bogus Sunday 'Christianese' and He said to me *"It starts with you!"* As I contemplated this, the idea for a weekly devotional based on transparency in my own life formed. It would mean that I would be exposed. It would mean I would have to risk being hurt and judged but I recognised that my life was *'no longer my own'* and that He was asking me to rise above my fear of rejection and trust Him. I would do it afraid... and so the *'Femail Encourager'* was born.

When I started the *'Femail Encourager'* I thought I was *'doing it for God to bless the women'*. What I realised at the end of 12 months was that God was doing it *'for me'*.

So, as I laboured and disciplined myself every Thursday evening to sit and write each one, He began to teach me, refine me, expand my thinking and bring my very being into line with His heart. I experienced first-hand the implications of **Hebrews 4:12** and I praise Him for His Word.

"For the Word of God is living and powerful, and sharper than any two-edged sword, piercing even to the division of soul and spirit, and of joints and marrow, and is a discerner of the thoughts and intents of the heart."
Hebrews 4:12

As the truth of His Word continues to expand my heart, He continues to prune and trim and challenge me and as I grow and surrender myself to His will, He asks more of me. I am often tired and the mountains seem huge but He orders my steps, He opens doors I never have to push, He goes before me and in it all I see promise and joy. I want to serve Him. My life is His alone. Whatever He asks I will do. Wherever He leads I will follow-*even to the desert places, even to the Valley of Achor.* For I know that without him my life amounts to nothing more than vanity. In Him I will live and in Him I will die and by His grace I will run this race until completion.

"For to me, to live is Christ, and to die is gain."
Philippians 1:21

The final chapter in this book is not so much a devotion but a workshop. Recently God said to me *"It is no longer enough just to feed the women, I want you to teach them to fish."* The study framework in this final chapter was born of this word to my heart. He has given me a desire to teach as many women as possible how to study and apply His Word using the same principals the Holy Spirit showed me during the season of writing the *'Femail Encourager'.* I pray that you will use this framework and as you do, the truth of His Word will become real in your heart and in your life. That as you seek after Him, He would reveal to you His purposes and that as He does, you would have the confidence to trust in Him and step out in faith, *despite* the waves that threaten.

> *"So then, faith comes by hearing and*
> *hearing by the WORD OF GOD."*
> **Romans 10:17**

I pray that the Holy Spirit might use these devotions and reflections to inspire and encourage you. That you would seek Him with all your heart, totally surrendered to his will and willing to submit and be moulded by the Potters Hand, into a vessel of great worth to His kingdom.

Remember... if you want to walk on water—*you need to get out of the boat!*

Acknowledgements

It would be impossible to thank everyone who has impacted my life and the writings you now find within the pages of this book–their names and faces span over a lifetime. There are so many individuals who have supported, protected, encouraged, challenged and inspired me. I thank each of you for your faithfulness.

There are others through whom God has taught me hard lessons and whose presence in my life has shaped character that could only be formed in the *'furnace of affliction'*. I thank you also, for I have come to understand that even the dark places have purpose and their existence enables me to fully appreciate and embrace the light.

There is one person I would like to acknowledge specifically. A woman whose gentle grace and capacity for love, has nurtured and inspired me more than any other. Who, despite her own hardship opened her heart and her home to a young pregnant stranger, never once blinking at the tattered, stinking 'baggage' that filed in after her.

We have laughed together, hurt together, grown as adults together. She has seen the worst of me and the best of me and remains a rare and treasured *'constant'* in my life. She is my most avid supporter, my *'Editor in Chief'*–my lifelong confidante and friend.

Thank you, Paula, for seeing me through the eyes of Jesus.

WEEK 1

ONE TREE AT A TIME

Scripture of the week

Philippians 3:13-14 *"...but one thing I do, forgetting those things which are behind and reaching forward to those things which are ahead, I press toward the goal for the prize of the upward call of God in Christ Jesus."*

Prayer of the week

Lord, when the enormity of the task before me fills my heart with fear and doubt, may I turn my eyes towards You. Grant me the grace to face each day, each minute fully dependant on Your strength and guidance. Teach me to be content with the manna You provide with each new dawn, knowing that Your provision is perfect... never too much, never too little. Help me Lord to focus only on those things You wish for me to do... nothing more, nothing less. Provide me with wisdom and grant me strength to let go of worry and concerns before I retire each evening. For Your Word says that *"sufficient for the day is its own trouble."* You are in control. **AMEN**

Felicity Eagan

Thought of the week
One tree at a time

Philippians 4:13 *"I can do all things through Christ who strengthens me."*

Step by Step

"He does not lead me year by year, Nor even day by day,
But step by step my path unfolds; My Lord directs my way."
(from the poem *'Step by Step'* by Barbara Ryberg)

After many months of studying, I decided to take a day just to 'relax' and regroup. For me, that meant getting outdoors and expending some pent up energy. And what better way to burn off some energy than to take a 26+ km bike ride along a scenic rail trail? Right?

I started out with the zest of an Olympic cyclist and I must admit for the most part, the ride was fairly easy going and enjoyable (which is probably fortunate given my limited fitness). I felt appropriately challenged but not overwhelmed–that is until I reached the final 2 km of the first leg at which point my energy and enthusiasm were both waning greatly.

The trail shown in the photo looks to be relatively flat, but don't be deceived. I stood at the bottom of this stretch and gazed towards the horizon and almost turned back. I looked at the path ahead with dread. The steady rise continued for what seemed to me an exceptionally vast distance and I just wasn't sure that I had the energy or fortitude to make it. My knees were hurting, my neck had a crick in it and my backside? Well let's just say bike seats are not the most comfortable of possies. It would require stamina and determination to push through and I just wasn't sure I had it.

So began an internal dialogue with myself that might have been of concern to anyone watching. Give in? Give up? Admit defeat? Turn around and go back? Or press on and rise to the challenge? With new found determination, I decided to press on and as I pressed on, I learned a valuable lesson. *(Praise the Lord... school's in even when I'm officially off duty!)*. Tentatively I hopped back onto the seat and pushed the pain to the back of my mind. I purposely concentrated on my breathing and the immediate task of pushing one pedal in front of the other, but after several minutes I looked up only to discover that the horizon appeared no closer. My heart sank and I became discouraged. I was nearly there and I could see the finish line, so close and yet so far. The final 2 kilometres seemed insurmountable. I was never going to make it! I'm just not fit enough!

Then came that little voice…*"just focus on getting to the next tree".* So that is what I did. I peddled that track, **one tree at a time**. The distance to the destination never changed, but something happened when I broke the journey down and focused only on reaching the next tree. The overall distance become less ominous and with each small accomplishment I became increasingly heartened. I was capable of believing that I could reach the next tree. The next tree *was* attainable and so before I knew it there I was, standing at the top of that seemingly 'insurmountable' rise taking the photo that you see above.

I had not only conquered the 'mountain' (even though technically it was nothing more than an incline), ***'precept upon precept, line upon line'***, (tree upon tree) ***(Isaiah 28:10)***, but at the end of the journey I was rewarded with the discovery of a lovely café that treated me with a hot latte and a delicious gluten free pie! I would have missed out on that fabulous reward had I given in to doubt and pain causing me to turn back and give up. God never promised that the journey would be easy or without doubt or pain or temptation. He never said it would be an easy ride. In fact Jesus said the exact opposite in **Matthew 16:24** *"... if anyone desires to come after me, let him deny himself and take up his cross and follow me."*

May you press on toward the goal and for the prize of the upward call of God in Christ Jesus for...

> *"Blessed is the man who endures temptation; for when he has been approved; he will receive the crown of life which the Lord has promised to those who love Him."*
> **James 1:12**

WEEK 2

A WORD IN SEASON

Scripture of the week

Proverbs 16:13 *"Righteous lips are the delight of kings, and they love him who speaks what is right."*

Prayer of the week

Lord, help me to be a person that builds others up. Teach me to speak words that bring life and encouragement. Let my heart beat with the rhythm of Your voice and let my words reflect Your heart. Teach me to *'deliver hard truths with grace'* and compassion and help me to identify those things that are true, noble, just, pure, lovely, of good report, virtuous and praiseworthy. In Jesus name. **AMEN**

Psalm 19:14 *"Let the words of my mouth and the meditation of my heart be acceptable in Your sight, O Lord, my strength and my Redeemer."*

Thought of the week
Words of life

A timely word of encouragement can mean the difference between hope and despair and I am beginning to understand more deeply that when God prompts I need to share that word He has placed on my heart. I have been surprised and humbled how often God pours out encouragement and blessing to others as a result of one simple act of obedience.

Quite often I will be driving along and the name of a person and then a scripture (or part of a scripture) will drop into my heart. Initially, I was confused by what this meant but as I have grown in the Lord I have come to understand that this is a gift that He has bestowed upon me and He is asking me to be His hands and feet and mouthpiece. Initially it brought fear and trepidation to my heart but as I have stepped out in obedience to His voice and delivered each word, I have seen the blessing and encouragement that has resulted.

Most often the words I get are those that gently encourage or bring confirmation, but on the odd occasion I have had to deliver a word of caution. Proceeding with great care, I have tried to be very sensitive in *'when'* and *'how'* I delivered these. I have pestered God for multiple confirmations to gain confirmation that I have heard Him correctly—it is one thing to make a mistake when delivering a word of encouragement, it is quite another to incorrectly deliver one that has the potential to do harm.

Fortunately on the occasions I have had to do this, the Holy Spirit has gone before me and prepared the heart of the person and they have acknowledged and expressed gratitude to God for *'seeing'* them and caring enough to speak truth of His Word into their lives.

Have you ever received a word and felt it was for someone and then been afraid to deliver, it only to find that God uses someone else to bless that person and often *'word for word'*—with the same message He gave you? I have! It is disappointing to say the least. This however, is not a message designed to incriminate but to encourage you to step out when God speaks to your heart.

A <u>positive</u> word of gentle encouragement might just be the difference between hope and despair in the life of another.

A word of advice

Please take care if the message you have is one of caution. Before delivering it, carefully examine your motivations and relationship with that person. Pray and ask God for multiple confirmations and ensure that it lines up with what His word says. If it doesn't, it is not of God and should be discarded.

When we are obedient to God's voice we become a conduit through which His grace is displayed to those who are struggling, to those who don't know Him and to those who are seeking His guidance.

May His name be praised and may His glory be evident in our lives as He empowers us with wisdom and courage to do the work He has called us to.

Finally, brethren,
whatever things *are* **true,**
whatever things *are* **noble,**
whatever things *are* **just,**
whatever things *are* **pure,**
whatever things *are* **lovely,**
whatever things *are* **of good
report,** if *there* is any virtue
and if *there* is anything praiseworthy,
meditate on these things.
Philippians 4:8

WEEK 3

HOPE WITH SUBSTANCE

Scripture of the week

Jeremiah 29:11 *"For I know the thoughts I think toward you, says the Lord, thoughts of peace and not of evil, to give you a future and a hope."*

Prayer of the week

Lord, thank You so much for the blessings You have provided in my life. I have so much and I know that it is because of You. You provide me with assurance of a future full of Your love and guidance and I know that no matter how bad things get, You are always by my side. I may not always see You or feel You, but it is at these times that I hold fast to the promises You gave me through Your Word, which tells me over and over again that You will never leave me or forsake me.

You knew me Lord even before I was formed in the womb. You know my dreams Lord and the deep desires of my heart. I place my dreams safely in Your hands, for You to mould and fit into the model of Your will and purpose for my life. I surrender my hopes and my dreams to You. **AMEN**

Thought of the week
Hope with substance

Hope: The definition of hope *reads 'confident expectation'* or *'firm assurance'* of things that are unclear and unknown. Biblical hope is what I call *'hope with substance'* because is based on the promises and truths of God's Word.

Faith: *"faith is the <u>substance</u> of things <u>hoped</u> for, the <u>evidence</u> of things unseen"* **Hebrews 11:1 (NKJV)** or *"faith is being <u>sure</u> of what we <u>hope</u> for, and <u>certain</u> of what we do not see"* **Hebrews 11:1 (NIV).**

Hope is the beginning of faith—it is the <u>expectation</u> that God's promises <u>will</u> be fulfilled in our lives. Hope is *'the potential'*—faith is *'the reality'* or the claimed ownership of the promises. That is, faith is the act of walking in the promises of what we know is possible even *before* we can evidence them as existing.

Psalm 37:4-5 *"Delight yourself also in the Lord, and He shall give you the desires of your heart. <u>Commit your way to the Lord,</u> trust also in Him and He shall bring it to pass."* (Emphasis mine).

Does this mean that God is going to give us everything we want? Certainly not! God does not cultivate spoilt brats!

The key is to **<u>commit your way to the Lord,</u>** then through the process of meditation on His Word and prayerful consideration, the dreams that develop within your heart will be in line with His will—these are Godly desires. This *seed of hope* that is planted in your heart will by *faith* take root and grow until it matures and produces fruit.

Godly desires are those placed in our hearts by God and are always in line with His will. These desires when passed under the microscope of His Word, will stand true against its scrutiny. It is these hopes that are candidates for reality, brought into existence through faith.

When our desires are in line with God's will then we can have *'confident expectation'* that He will bring them to pass... this is the foundation of Hope.

> *"Show me Your ways, O Lord; teach me Your paths.*
> *Lead me in Your truth and teach me, for*
> *You are the God of my salvation;*
> *On You I wait all the day."*
> **Psalm 25:4-5**

WEEK 4

MARTHA! MARTHA! MARTHA!

Scripture of the week

Psalm 46:10 *"Be still and know that I am God; I will be exalted among the nations, I will be exalted on the earth!"*

Prayer of the week

Lord help me to listen to Your voice. Forgive me for the times I let the busyness of life get in the way of hearing Your voice. Help me to not miss the signs that You place in my path to guide me. Signs that when ignored put me out of Your will and on the path of danger. Teach me to sit at your feet and listen just as Mary did. To revel in the love and wisdom that you desire to impart into my life and that as I wait on You, my strength might be renewed. **AMEN**

Thought of the week

Enter into My rest

This was the word the Lord gave me... I didn't listen. In fact I didn't even recognise that it was for me. To make matters worse I sent it on thinking it was for someone else (who was just a little puzzled when I did). In short, *I got it wrong!*

A few days later, I fell in a heap... so much so I could barely keep my eyes open, let alone focus on my work. I had been ignoring all the signs and pushing myself beyond my capacity to reasonably cope and it took all my determination that day not to crawl under my desk and fall asleep. I was exhausted physically and emotionally and *God knew.*

In fact, He knows me so well that he knew He would have to virtually hit me over the head before I would turn from my Martha ways and sit at His feet and listen. Yesterday He got my attention.

In the course of the day I received the verse *"Be still and know that I am God"* several times via several different means and all non-related. God was telling me to stand still and listen. **He had something important to tell me.**

Finally I stood still and I listened, and have since made the resolution I should have made earlier—to heed His voice. How easily I could have missed the opportunity for God to minister to me.

I pray that each of us will discipline ourselves to stop and be still... to take the time to sit at the feet of Jesus and just listen.

John 10:27 *"My sheep hear my voice, and **I know them**, and they follow me."*

> *Praise God, He is wise,*
> *Praise God, He knows our needs,*
> *Praise God, He is longsuffering,*
> *May He be exalted in our lives.*

WEEK 5

THE VALLEY OF ACHOR

Scripture of the week

Habakkuk 3:19 *"The Lord God is my strength; He will make my feet like hind's feet and He will make me to walk upon my high hills."*

Prayer of the week

Lord, teach me to sacrifice my will for Yours. Give me the courage to stay on the narrow path and within the safety of Your will even when the wider path appears easier to travel. Help me to cast down imaginations and any high thing that would come between us and what I know of You to be true. Teach me to trust when it appears that my only companions are sorrow and suffering. Help me to trust in You even when the way is unfamiliar. **AMEN**

Thought of the week

As 'surefooted' as a deer

When I read the verse in *Habakkuk 3:19* it took my memory back to a book that was given to me many years ago. The book was called *'Hinds Feet on High Places'* by *Hannah Hurnard*.

The book is an allegory (a story with a hidden meaning) and regales the journey of a fictional character known simply as *'Much-Afraid'*.

Much-Afraid heeds the call of the *'Chief Shepherd'* (Jesus) who sows the seed of Divine Love in her heart so that it might grow and blossom into 'perfect love' (which casts out fear). Through His encouragement, she then embarks on a journey up a rocky mountain top to reach the *'High Places'* where she hopes to find fulfilment outside the harping voices and menacing actions of her relatives who live in the *'Valley of Humiliation'*.

The Shepherd travels with her only a short distance and then allows her to go forward whilst he watches over her and gives aid when she calls. He gives her two guides to help her ascend the mountain, their names are *'Sorrow and Suffering'* and they are to be her companions on the journey.

The story goes on to tell how the relatives whose names include, *'Pride, Resentment, Bitterness and Self Pity'* try to discourage and manipulate her into turning back and yoking herself in marriage to *'Craven-Fear'*, her previously betrothed.

Along the way Much-Afraid discovers the unexpected beauty of wild-flowers such as *'Acceptance with Joy'* and *'Bearing the Cost'* and as she overcomes each trial and submits her will to that of the Shepherd, she builds an altar of sacrifice and collects a memorial stone to remember each lesson learned.

In her travels she will detour *'through the desert'*, wander the *'shores of the sea of loneliness'*, encounter *'opposition and injury'*, weather the *'storm of tribulation'* and navigate her way through the *'mist of uncertainty'* and it is through these experiences that she learns to trust and call on the Shepherd for strength and guidance. Finally, she surrenders her total will to His leading and it is here that she enters the *'place of anointing'*.

At this stage of the journey she takes the final steps to her death... the death of her own will. In this death to self and resurrection to the will of God, *'Sorrow and Suffering'* are transformed into *'Joy and Peace'*; the memorial stones she has collected are transformed into jewels from which will be fashioned her heavenly crown and; Much-Afraid herself is bestowed a new name more in line with her transformation brought about by the journey, *'Glory and Grace'*.

Wrapping it up

The theme of the book is about crucifying your own will for that of Christ. Every time you resolve to crucify those parts of yourself that are un-glorifying to God, you are offering an altar of sacrifice and through this act of submission comes spiritual maturity and growth, resulting in the development of *'hinds feet'* that will enable you to stand steadfast. Just as the mountain deer are surefooted on the towering precipices of the high places, you too will be able to scale the rocky precipices you encounter with grace, agility and steadfastness. *"Let His Grace be sufficient for you for His strength is made perfect in your weakness."* **(see 2 Corinthians 12:9).**

Hosea 2:14-15 *"Therefore, behold I will allure her, will bring her into the wilderness, and speak comfort to her. I will give her, her vineyards from there, and the* **Valley of Achor (trouble)** *as a door of hope; she shall sing there, as in the days of her youth, as in the day when she came up from the land of Egypt."*

I pray that as you travel through the valleys in your life, you will know that God is always present, encouraging you to grow and mature and develop hinds feet, so that you can navigate the precipices of His calling with 'Grace', 'Agility' and 'Steadfastness'.

WEEK 6

THE PURSUIT OF HAPPYNESS

Scripture of the week

Matthew 6:19–21 "*Do not lay up for yourselves treasure on earth, where moth and rust destroy and where thieves break in and steal; but lay up for yourselves treasures in heaven, where neither moth nor rust destroys and where thieves do not break in and steal.* **For where your treasure is, there your heart is also.**"

Prayer of the week

Lord, I pray that as I journey through this world that my thoughts, prayers, actions and motivations would be such that they have an eternal focus. Help me not to be insular, getting caught up in placing too much importance on those things that have no eternal value. Help me instead to meditate and focus on those things that have eternal worth, things that will extend Your kingdom and bring Glory to Your Name.

Father, **use me** as an instrument of Your righteousness here on earth. I pray that as my heart desires to seek first Your kingdom that Your joy will be made full in me and that this Fruit of the Spirit will shine as a beacon to those who are lost. **AMEN**

Thought of the week
The pursuit of 'happyness'

For much of my life I have been searching... *searching* for purpose, *searching* for understanding but most of all *searching* for something that seemed unattainable–*happiness*.

This is what I have discovered...
The world will tell you that happiness comes from *having*... *having* things, *having* friends, *having* well behaved children, *having* a great job, *having* a goal, *having* a great marriage, *having* a loving childhood... just *having* in general.

Others will tell you that happiness comes from *within* and to attain it we only need to unlock the hidden joy within. So, in my avid search I explored this also and read every self-help book on the *"key to happiness"* that existed in libraries and bookstores from here to the Amazons, *to no avail*. Despite every attempt I made I just wasn't able to conjure up or find that elusive key to happiness (ie. the true happiness that satisfied the cravings of my soul). *Lots of promises*–no real deliveries!

In the end I was left feeling dissatisfied, empty, depressed and *without hope*...

I have come to understand that neither of the above will ever lead to happiness. In fact both are rooted in SELF–*self gain, self focus, self gratification* and *self*

***sufficiency*.** When we focus on SELF we take our eyes away from God and in doing this we raise ourselves up as idols.

Praise God this is not the end of the story!

> ***True joy comes from God and being in***
> ***right relationship with Him...***
> *"You will show me the path of life;*
> *In Your presence is fullness of joy;*
> *At Your right hand are pleasures forevermore."*
> **Psalm 16:11**

> ***True joy comes from walking in the Spirit...***
> *"But the fruit of the Spirit is love, JOY, peace,*
> *patience, kindness, goodness, faithfulness and self-control."*
> **Galatians 5:22**

> ***Happiness and Joy are not the same ...***
> Happiness is an event dependent on circumstances.
> Joy is the smile we hold in our heart no
> matter what is going on around us.

The Apostle Paul says..."***But I REJOICED in the Lord greatly*** that now at last your care for me has flourished again; though you surely did care, but you lacked opportunity. Not that I speak in regard to need, ***for I have learned in whatever state I am to be content.***" ***Philippians 4:10-11*** (Emphasis mine).

The **KEY:**

"If you keep My commandments you will abide in My love, just as I have kept my Fathers commandments and abide in His love. These things I have spoken to you, that MY JOY may remain in you, and that your JOY may be full." John 15:10-11 (Emphasis mine).

Jesus is the source of all JOY and by keeping His commandments and abiding in His love we may walk in the fullness of HIS joy. Seek the kingdom (eternal focus) and you will receive the JOY of the Lord!

The **COMMANDMENT:**

"This is my commandment, that you love one another as I have loved you." John 15:12

The **REWARD:**

(The Parable of the Talents) - *"His lord said to him, "Well done, good and faithful servant, You have been faithful over a few things, I will make you ruler over many things. Enter into the JOY of your lord." Matthew 25:21*

My prayer for you

"Now may the God of hope fill you with all JOY and peace in believing, that you may abound in hope (not hopelessness) *by the power of the Holy Spirit." Romans 15:13*

ON'T BE DECEIVED

ripture of the week

John 10:10 *"The thief does not come except to steal, and to kill and to destroy. I have come that they may have life and that they may have it more abundantly."*

Prayer of the week

Abba, Father... thank you that I am a child of the King and that through the sacrifice of Your only begotten Son, I have the privilege of inheriting the promises contained in Your Word. Help me to remember to claim the promises You have given me, to take hold of my true identity in You and to resist the Devil that he would not gain a foothold in my life or thoughts. Protect me, that I would not be deceived by lies but liberated by truth–Your truth.

Thank you that You see beyond the *'now'* to the bigger picture, that You have every aspect of my life in Your control and that I need not fear or become anxious but only trust in Your goodness and purpose for my life. Your will be done Lord, on Earth as it is in Heaven. **AMEN**

Thought of the week
Don't be deceived

"The thief comes to steal, kill and destroy..." **(see John 10:10)**

Do you ever have those weeks when you wish your life was a cassette tape and you could rewind, delete and start again?

At times, I have be plagued by a battle in my mind and swamped by a barrage of negative thoughts and attitudes that have been stimulated by a steady flow of disappointments, let-downs and uncertainties.

All the old fears, reactions and insecurities creep in and threaten to immobilise me. Feelings that I am reaching above my station; that I am living in the land of the fairies and any moment my world is going to topple down on top of me and bring me crashing back down to Earth again. I won't even get started on the topic of my struggle with *"consider the lilies of the field."* **(see Matthew 6:28)**

What I really need when I am in this place is an Olympic swimming pool to contain my self-pity puddle!

Stand firm on the word and the truth contained therein

"I have come that they may have life and that they may have it more abundantly."

It sometimes takes me a little while but I eventually realise what is happening. The Devil is using me to have a field day and for some reason I just stand there and let him.

Ephesians 6:16 *"Above all, taking the shield of faith with which you will be able to quench all the fiery darts of the wicked one."*

The TRUTH is that my identity and circumstances are not defined by what I see through my limited vision and understanding but through Christ I am a joint-heir to the promises of the King.

Romans 8:15-17 *"For you did not receive the spirit of bondage again to fear, but you received the Spirit of adoption by who we cry out, 'Abba, Father'. The Spirit Himself bears witness with our spirit that we are children of God, and if children, then heirs—heirs of God and joint heirs with Christ, if indeed we suffer with Him, that we may also be glorified together."*

2 Corinthians 5:7 *"For we walk by FAITH, not by sight."*

If God said it… if it's in His Word, I believe it! For His Word is TRUTH.

The Promises

A small sample of some of God's promises we can claim as joint heir kids…

"For God has not given us a Spirit of fear but of power and of love and of a sound mind." ***2 Timothy 1:7***

"Give and it will be given to you; good measure, pressed down, shaken together and running over, will be poured into your bosom." **Luke 6:38a**

"He who has a generous eye will be blessed, for he gives his bread to the poor." **Proverbs 22:9**

"God is our refuge and strength, a very present help in trouble." **Psalm 46:1**

"He gives power to the weak and to those who have no might He increases strength." **Isaiah 40:29**

"My sheep listen to My voice, I know them and they follow Me. And I give them eternal life, and they shall never perish; neither shall anyone snatch them out of My hand." **John 10:27-28**

"Be anxious for nothing, but in everything by prayer and supplication, with thanksgiving, let your requests be made known to God, and the peace of God, which surpasses all understanding, will guard your hearts and minds through Christ Jesus." **Philippians 4:6-7**

"Now this is the confidence that we have in Him, that if we ask anything according to His will, He hears us." **1 John 5:14**

"When you pass through the waters, I will be with you; and through the rivers, they shall not overflow you. When you walk through the fire, you shall not be burned; nor shall the flame scorch you." **Isaiah 43:1-2**

Proverbs 3:5-6 *"Trust in the Lord with all your heart and lean not on your own understanding; in all your ways acknowledge Him, and He shall direct your paths."*

I am certain that there are times in each of our lives that we unwittingly succumb to the lies that the enemy would have us believe about ourselves. It is times like this that we need to take up our shield of faith (believe Gods Word and not the circumstances before us) and fight back with the sword of the Spirit (let the Devil know who you are in Christ, claim the promises of His Word).

For through Christ we are a new creation. When we resist the Devil and declare our identity in Christ, then he (the Devil) has no power or authority in our lives.

The face lift

- Pray without ceasing
- Bring a sacrifice of Praise to God
- Worship Him in Spirit and in Truth
- Verbally claim the promises of God's Word

I guarantee your countenance will shine afterwards.

My prayer for you

"So now, brethren, I commend you to God and to the word of His Grace, which is able to build you up and give you an inheritance among all those who are sanctified." **Acts 20:32**

WEEK 8

WATCH AND PRAY

Scripture of the week

Philippians 3:14 *"I press toward the goal for the prize of the upward call of God in Christ Jesus."*

Prayer of the week

Lord, You are the Creator of the heavens and the Earth. You created everything in it, including us. Yet so often we are intent on relegating You to the back closet of our lives. Father, You know our weaknesses, You know that the cares of this world often cloud our view and shift our focus from that which is important to that which is mere vanity and '*dust to the wind*'. Father, by your Spirit, convict me when I am becoming lukewarm. Rekindle the fire of my first love Lord, that I remain in intimate relationship with You. I praise You Lord for Your faithfulness, for Your wisdom, Your mercy and Your grace. **AMEN**

Thought of the week
Watch and pray

Recently I had to make a fairly major choice... to remain living where I was or to return to my home town... the place of my roots, *the place I felt comfortable.*

My new job was in my home town, my children, my sister, my old house, my old friends and *my memories...* it made good sense to move back.

But... as I drove around the streets, revelling in the nostalgia and thinking how *comfortable* and familiar it all was, I sensed God speak directly to my heart and the words stopped me in my tracks.

"I don't want you to be comfortable!"

Why! Why would God say that? I didn't understand and I struggled with the '*injustice*' of it for some time before I finally accepted it.

The reality is that God knows me better than I know myself. He knows that for me, '*comfortable*' translates to '*complacency*'. '*Complacency*' leads to '*familiarity*' and '*familiarity*' leads to '*contempt*'. The thing about contempt is that it *resists change*, it *hates being challenged* and it ultimately *anaesthetises one's willingness to be moved by suffering, to be an available vessel, to count the cost and to take up the cross of Christ*. He knows me well enough to know that a little discomfort in my life ensures my heart remains alert towards things that matter and that my eyes remain firmly focused on Him.

Complacency is enmity to the soul and left unchecked it will eventually lead to spiritual paralysis. The human quest for comfort inevitably numbs our senses enough that we become desensitized to the call of God in our lives and our focus turns from His purposes to that of our flesh.

One day, without even seeing it coming you wake up and realise that *"What was once first in your life, now becomes last"* and you have traded God's eternal blessings for temporary pleasure.

The Apostle Paul refers in **2 Corinthians 12:7** to the *'thorn in his flesh'*—the affliction that never allowed him to rest or become 'complacent' lest he fall victim to the sin of pride. It caused him to remain close to and in the will of God. He understood that this thorn was for but a short time and he was willing to endure temporary discomfort for the hope of eternity and the Glory of God.

The Biblical take on complacency

God's word to the Prophet Zephaniah warns God's people about their complacency and lack of reverence towards God...

Zephaniah 1:12 *"And it shall come to pass at that time that I will search Jerusalem with lamps and punish the men who are settled in complacency, who say in their heart the Lord will not do good, nor will He do evil."*

A similar warning is heralded in by Amos...
Amos 6:3-7 *"Woe to you who put far off the day of doom, who cause the seat of violence to come near who lie on beds of ivory, stretch out on your couches, eat lambs from the*

flock and calves from the midst of the stall; who sing idly to the sound of stringed instruments, and invent for yourselves musical instruments like David; who drink wine from bowls, and anoint yourselves with the best ointments, but are not grieved for the affliction of Joseph. Therefore they shall now go captive as the first of the captives, and those who recline at Banquets shall be removed."

And in Revelation, Jesus Himself reminds us...
Revelation 3:15-17 *"I know your works, that you are neither cold nor hot. I wish you were cold or hot. So then, because you are lukewarm and neither cold nor hot, I will vomit you out of My mouth. Because you say 'I am rich, have become wealthy, and have need of nothing'—and do not know that you are wretched, miserable, poor, blind and naked."*

Ouch!... how's that for discomfort?

The Victory is in Christ

God is a just God and the Bible is full of consequences for sin and strategies as to how to avoid it. As we grow and develop in our faith there will be times when we fail but God in His mercy is waiting to lift us up and guide us through the quagmire of our own folly, to provide wise counsel in order that we might grow in faith. God does not expect that we will not fail, only that we look to Him for strength in our weakness. His mercy is new every morning.

Spiritual Complacency requires **Spiritual Inoculation...**

- Be Transformed by the renewing of your mind *(see Romans 12:2 | Ephesians 4:23)*
- Meditate on things that are noble and of good report *(see Philippians 4:8)*
- Examine yourself and your faith *(see 2 Corinthians 13:5)*
- Watch and pray lest you fall into temptation *(see Matthew 26:41)*
- Work out your salvation in fear and trembling *(see Philippians 2:12)*
- Confess your sins and seek forgiveness *(see 1 John 1:9)*

So, run the race in such a way as to win the prize which promises eternal rewards.
(see 1 Corinthians 9:24-27)

WEEK 9

THE FULLER'S SOAP

Scripture of the week

Malachi 3:2 *"But who can endure the day of His coming? And who can stand when He appears? For He is like a refiner's fire and like fuller's soap."*

Prayer of the week

Lord, refine me and prove me that through the testing of my faith I will be able to stand strong in times of tribulation. I pray that by Your Spirit and through the transforming power of Your Word I would be cleansed and renewed. Lord, I offer myself as a living sacrifice to You, cleanse me from all unrighteousness. For the glory of your name. **AMEN**

Thought of the week

<u>**Quote:**</u>
"For most of us knowledge is not the bridge to growth ... pain is."
(Anonymous)

Lord, send me to the cleaners!

You could be forgiven for thinking, based on this week's scripture that my topic would be on the work of the refiner's fire. Indeed, originally my plan was to take you on a tour of the Refiners Workshop and to woo you with promises of *precious metals* but instead God gives me, **SOAP!**

In all fairness, the Refiner's Fire was exactly the subject I had in mind but as I pondered the verse from Malachi my eyes kept returning to the words *'Fuller's Soap'*... and I found myself wondering *"What exactly does that mean?"*

So, sorry girls despite my best intentions, today we take a trip to the laundry...

A new perspective on laundry

In Biblical times, the Fuller was responsible for cleaning and *'thickening'* new fibres and freshly woven garments through a process of cleaning, bleaching, wetting and beating the cloth fibres until they attained the *desired condition*. **Fuller's soap** was an important alkali substance (*active ingredient*) used in this process and was derived from plant ashes (pot ash) mixed with a fatty substance to produce soap. A number of other ingredients including putrid urine were used in the process, can you imagine the smell!

On this basis I am secretly pleased to know that the Fuller was a **man's** profession! (I would be very interested if anyone knows how this role of laundry just casually transferred to **woman**!)

The reference in Malachi to the **'Fuller's soap'** and the role of the **Fuller** in the *'**fulling** of a garment'* refers to an ancient Jewish practice which also holds profound spiritual relevance. It is a spiritual metaphor which I have tried to explain in the following diagram... *hopefully it makes sense!*

God loves us enough to stretch us and prove us that we might stand strong in our faith in times of trouble and uncertainty...

1 Peter 1:6-7 *"In this you greatly rejoice, though now for a little while, if need be, you have been distressed by various trials, that the genuineness of your faith, being much more precious than gold that perishes, though it is tested by fire, may be found to praise, honour, and glory at the revelation of Jesus Christ."*

and in the words of Job... who knew the fullers process well!

"But He knows the way that I take; when He has tested me, I shall come forth as gold. My foot has held fast to His steps; I have kept His way and not turned aside."
Job 23:10-11

The Fullers' Process

Fibres are sent to the Fuller

They are in a terrible state-full of oil and grimy substances-*dull, lifeless and grubby!*

Fibres

We are the raw fibre-dirty and sinful-*dull, lifeless and grubby!*

The fibres undergo the 'Fullers' process

Soaked in water mixed with putrid urine, clay, *fullers soap (active ingredient)* -very smelly and unsavoury process!

The fibres are beaten on a flat rock using a stone or paddle-over and over and over again until the fabric *'fills out'* and *'gains substance'* and attains the *'desired condition'*.

Jesus is the Fuller

He takes the raw materials (us) and guides them through a harrowing process of proving and conditioning in order to test our 'mettle' and produce *'substance'* and a *'desired condition'* so that we become suitable to fulfil our purpose.

The *'active ingredient'*-or the Holy Spirit (fullers' soap) makes the transformation possible.

The fibres are repeatedly washed

In order to purify the fibres and remove the residual dirt, smell and impurities... the result of which is a pure white fabric-*free from stain and blemish* and ready for its Holy purpose (religious ceremony)

The fibres are repeatedly washed

The washing of the garment is the truth and cleansing that comes about through the power of the Gospel in our lives and from immersing our minds in the transforming power of God's Word.

The result is spiritual cleansing that prepares us that we might be an offering of righteousness to be used for a Holy purpose... *God's call on our lives.*

WEEK 10

WISDOM IS THE PRINCIPAL THING!

Scripture of the week

Proverbs 3:5-6 *"Trust in the Lord with all your heart and lean not on your own understanding. In all your ways acknowledge Him and He shall direct your paths."*

Prayer of the week

Lord show me Your will, keep me on the right path. Teach me to trust You as the source of my salvation. Lead me and guide me always. Give me Your direction. Give me patience to wait until You're ready for me. Train me to follow after You in everything I do. Let me know Your wisdom. Enlighten my soul to Your every prompting. Encompass me in Your passion, until our hearts become one. **AMEN**

Thought of the week
Wisdom is the principal thing!

The more I learn, the more I realise how little I actually know. As I journey through life I understand more and more that to trust in the blinkered view of my own wisdom is perhaps the most foolish thing I have ever done.

I would have spared myself much of the despair and pain I have endured if only I had trusted *God more* and *me less*.

Divine wisdom is a gift from God

Godly wisdom does not operate within the limitations of our human understanding and *'worldly wisdom'*. Worldly wisdom is formulated from our *experiences* and *learned* knowledge. It is the product of *'cause'* and *'effect'* and is restricted by our narrow view of the world and our fractional interpretation of it.

Godly wisdom however, is without limitations. It is not partial in its knowing but perfect and whole. It is not based on learning or experience but its beginning and its end is found in the divine nature of God. Godly wisdom is not learned, it was from the beginning. God IS knowledge, God IS wisdom, He is I AM and He IS omniscient (all knowing).

And... through Christ this wisdom is available to us as believers.

The wisdom of The Creator far exceeds that of the created!

The Bible is full of references to wisdom and the desirability of attaining it. To the unbeliever, Godly wisdom is often seen as foolish but to those who have the mind of Christ and understanding through spiritual discernment, Godly wisdom is the foundation of 'truth' that brings fullness of life.

Proverbs 16:25 *"There is a way that seems right to a man but its' end is the way of death."*

Tapping in to the wisdom of God

"For precept must be upon precept, precept upon precept, line upon line, line upon line. Here a little, there a little." **Isaiah 28:10**

For most of us the ability to tap into and consistently walk in the wisdom of God is not instantaneous, rather it is progressive. As we exchange the milk of infants for the meat that comes with spiritual maturity, Godly wisdom and spiritual discernment increases and human wisdom decreases.

Proverbs 4:7 *"Wisdom is the principal thing; therefore get wisdom. And in all your getting, get understanding."*

How?

Seek it with all your heart from within the depths of God's Word...

As believers we are empowered through the Holy Spirit who dwells in us, to discern the truths contained within the pages of the Bible, the Word of God. To the unbeliever the Bible is a book of stories, to the believer the Bible is living and dynamic and it contains the keys to fulfilment and fullness of life. *(see 1 Corinthians 2: 13-14)*

Practice spiritual discernment by listening to <u>and</u> acting on the promptings of the Holy Spirit...
Hebrews 5:14 *"But solid food belongs to those who are full of age that is, those who by reason of use have their senses exercised to discern both good and evil."*

Acknowledge the limitations associated with human understanding and trust in the *"all knowing"* wisdom of God *even* when it doesn't make sense from where you stand...

"For the wisdom of this world is foolishness with God..." ***1 Corinthians 3:19a***

Fear God with a Holy reverence that inspires action and not just lip service... *for*

"The fear of the Lord is the <u>beginning</u> of wisdom..." ***Proverbs 9:10a***

- **Wisdom is *precious*,** more than pearls or gems or silver or gold ***(Proverbs 8:10-11)***
- **Wisdom *bestows blessings*,** of deliverance ***(Proverbs 28:26)***; strength ***(Proverbs 3:8)***; happiness ***(Proverbs 3:13)***; respect ***(Deuteronomy 4:6|Luke 2:52)*** and; it brings health to our flesh ***(Proverbs 3:8)***
- **Wisdom carries *a burden of responsibility*,** for with increased knowledge comes increased sorrow ***(Ecclesiastes 1:18)***; a mandate to walk uprightly ***(Ephesians 5:15)*** and; a heart to reach the

unsaved... "*he who wins souls is wise.*" **(Proverbs 11:30)**

"Do not be wise in your own eyes;
Fear the Lord and depart from evil. It will be health
to your flesh, And strength to your bones."
(Proverbs 3:7-8)

WEEK 11

STATE YOUR CASE AND REFUSE TO ARGUE

Scripture of the week

1 Thessalonians 5:21-22 *"Test all things; hold fast to what is good; abstain from every form of evil."*

Prayer of the week

Lord, teach me by Your Spirit to recognise that which is good and that which is evil. That which brings You glory and that which is based in pride or arrogance, that which is edifying and that which brings death. Father, give me the courage to choose and participate in that which is upright and Holy and may Your name be glorified in my life. **AMEN**

Thought of the week
Plant the seed and water with prayer

This week I spent some time with an old acquaintance. She is 'alternate and earthy'; she calls a spade a spade and says what she thinks... *my kind of person.*

To give you greater insight to our relationship, I met her during my years of being a 'non-practicing' Christian and we had this unspoken agreement not to talk about religion. She never asked me what I believed and I never made the effort to tell her nor did I ever challenge her new age thinking... as a result our relationship was easy and comfortable.

But this night was different... This night we spoke about faith... This night a wedge was placed between us...

This night my response to her questions and my explanation of the gospel and the path of salvation caused a rift between us. I pray it will be the beginning of her journey to repentance.

Ephesians 2:8-9 *"For by grace you have been **saved through faith**, and not of yourselves; it is the free gift of God, **not of works**, lest anyone should boast."*

You see, she believes she is a good person... she believes in *'a'* god but not *'the'* God of the Bible. She doesn't believe that the Bible is the divine Word of God nor does she believe that Jesus is the Son of God or the Messiah. In her eyes my believing the gospel of Christ was passing judgment on her by default and *"how dare I".*

The venom with which she referred to 'organised religion' was almost tangible and I realised that at some point she had been badly hurt. Her display of emotion was so intense that it was impossible to try and respond without being drowned out and spoken over and as her anger escalated I just sat there silently stunned at the intensity of her reaction.

Lord... what do I do?

As I whispered this silent prayer, the words that a Christian friend once shared with me dropped into my heart, **"State your case and refuse to argue."**

The peace that came over me was incredible and at that point I realised that nothing I could say would make a difference at this time. Her heart was closed to my words... I had planted the seed but faith and spiritual understanding would only come through the conviction of the Holy Spirit, I had to take my hands off and *let God.*

As Christians our calling is to show the love of Christ; to share the gospel of salvation and; to make disciples. It is the Holy Spirit that brings conviction and he uses the seeds we plant, the love we show the glory of creation and the miracle of grace to attain his purpose.

Conversion therefore is the final act and it is an act of *'free will'* by the unbeliever alone. It is the point at which *they* actively choose to humble themselves and recognise their need for salvation, the point at which *they* willingly turn their back on the old way of living and trust in Christ alone as their source.

God is able to bring the 'tuff nuts' to repentance...
Matthew 19:26 "*...with men this is impossible but with God all things are possible.*"

The fact that Paul, who actively and aggressively persecuted Christians, was touched and so radically convicted and transformed from an 'antagonistic' <u>unbeliever</u> to an 'uncompromising' <u>believer</u> is a powerful testimony to the life changing ability of the gospel. If God chose to remove the scales from Paul's eyes how much more able is he to remove them from the eyes of those we love and are called to love.

Do not argue, a Biblical stance

God has planted in us the capacity to be wise and to discern when someone is genuinely interested in hearing about the gospel or if they are arguing just for the sake of arguing. It is our mandate to share the gospel with the lost and to strengthen the saints but arguing with people whose intent is for nothing more than to discredit Christ, or to prove their point, is a relatively pointless exercise. There is far more value in praying for them than arguing with them.

It is not beneficial to speak of spiritual things to those who don't value it. I in the end, they will only use it against you. *"Do not give what is holy to the dogs; nor cast your pearls before swine, lest they trample them under their feet, and turn and tear you in pieces."* **Matthew 7:6**

Don't argue about the technicalities of words, such negativity brings doubt to those listening *"...not to strive about words to no profit, to the ruin of hearers."* **2 Timothy 2:14b**

Avoid worthless foolish talk, it is not beneficial and it spreads like cancer. *"But shun profane and idle babblings; for they will increase to more ungodliness. And their message will spread like cancer..."* **2 Timothy 2:16-17**

Don't get involved with foolish arguments, they only end up in fights. *"But avoid foolish and ignorant disputes, knowing that they generate strife."* **2 Timothy 2:23**

"Do not answer a fool according to his folly, lest you also be like him. Answer a fool according to his folly, lest he be wise in his own eyes". **Proverbs 26:4-5**. Although these verses seem to contradict each other they are actually quite profound.

v4–To argue with a fool on his own terms is often futile and you are at risk of stooping to his level when you do so. *However...*

v5–If a fool must be addressed, then take the fool's own words and use them to expose the folly of his reasoning thus causing him to recognise the foolishness of his argument.

WEEK 12

FRUIT WORTHY OF REPENTANCE

Scripture of the week

Matthew 3:8 | Luke 3:8 *"Therefore bear fruits worthy of repentance..."* (John the Baptist).

Prayer of the week

Lord, help me to stand up and be accountable and to not be ashamed of the truth of Your gospel. Your Word says that Christ came not to bring peace on earth but division. Help me as Your child to be proud of the heritage I have in You, and to declare Your Name regardless of popular opinion. Father by Your Spirit impart conviction that I might repent daily... that I might bear fruit worthy of repentance. In Jesus name. **AMEN**

Thought of the week
Where the rubber meets the road

I have been challenged this week with the words of these verses in Matthew and Luke. *"Therefore bear fruits worthy of repentance..."*

Are the attitudes, actions and out-workings of my life consistent with having <u>truly</u> *repented from sin*? John the

Baptist believed the gospel with such conviction and integrity that he was willing to endure all things, even prison and finally death.

Head knowledge is very different from heart knowledge. Head knowledge results in fear and arrogance and compliance... heart knowledge results in humility, repentance and <u>action</u> originating from a grateful heart love response.

Repentance is the act of turning from sin to God... it means to wilfully change your mind in such a way that it affects your <u>actions</u>.

I have spent many years being what I call a professional 'Christian Scholar' but very few actually believing the scriptures I read and learnt. It is a daily struggle for me. I doubt often, sin often and find myself confessing my failings time and again for things that should be finished, done and dusted. Yet I seem to continuously travel around the same mountain only to return to the point at which I began, no wiser and even worse, willing to blindly travel the same road and embark on the same lessons.

How many times must we travel the same path before we realise that it is within our power to break the cycle. To turn from the path before us onto the one less travelled... we *just need to* **change our mind.**

God's grace will uphold us when we fall but if we truly realised the depth of the pain we cause the Father each time we sin, perhaps then we would take more seriously our role in repentance.

There is a song by **Point of Grace** in which the final lines read: *"The secret to walking down life's road... is to believe what I already know."*

I wonder how willing we are to walk the reality of the words we profess when push comes to shove and the rubber meets the road.

Diminishing power

Repentance is a conscious choice of our mind and will and it is an ongoing process of choosing God over sin. The Holy Spirit in us provides us with the conviction of sin and the strength that underpins the 'decision' to turn from sin.

Every time you succeed in standing up for what you believe and not giving into temptation you become stronger in that conviction and one day you will realise that that particular mountain no longer holds any power over you.

When we repent, we change the focus from us to God. When our focus is on God, we think and act in a manner which is pleasing to Him and the natural out-working of this is *'fruit worthy of repentance'.*

True repentance results in Godly fruit *"but declared first to those in Damascus and in Jerusalem, and throughout all the region of Judea, and then to the Gentiles that they should repent, turn to God and do works befitting repentance."* **Acts 26:20**

What is 'Fruit worthy of Repentance'?

There are lots of examples in the Bible but I will focus on the examples given in *Luke Chapter 3* which gives us a pretty good clue...

Verse 11
"He who has two tunics let him give to him who has none and he who has food, let him do likewise."

Notice the verse doesn't say. Assess whether the candidate is worthy or appreciative of the gift and determine if they are going to use the tunic/food in a manner in which you approve. It is the act of grace, compassion and generosity and our obedience to the Word of God that should be the motivating factor. I have to remind myself of this one often.

Verse 13
"Collect no more than what is appointed to you."

Jesus was referring to the Tax Collectors, those that worked in a notoriously corrupt profession. His instruction to them was to deal fairly (in accordance with the law and moral justice), to take <u>no more</u> than what is appointed to em and to have integrity in their dealings. Man may not see acts of corruption... *God does.*

<u>Verse 14</u>
"Do not intimidate anyone or accuse falsely, and be content with your wages."

It is said that the hallmark of a great man is not that he has vast power but that he <u>chooses</u> not to unduly exercise it. The message here is to treat people fairly and with respect. Deliver a fair day's work for a fair day's pay and learn to be content where you are at, not always striving for bigger, better faster.

The potters shed...
A lady whose husband was a potter used to care for my son when he was a baby. One day I went to the shed and found him breaking up cracked unglazed pots that he had made and then putting them in a bucket which he then covered with water. He told me that after a few days the water softens the clay again and he is able to re-use it to create a new and perfect pot that can be fired, glazed and made usable. God takes us, broken and hard and gradually softens us until we reach a point in which we are pliable and then He can remould us and create a beautiful, usable vessel.

How do we bear 'Fruit worthy of Repentance'?

Repent and turn from self focus to God focus. It is at this point that our lives will produce fruit befitting repentance.

WEEK 13

THE WINDS OF GOD

Scripture of the week

Psalm 48:7 *"Thou breakest the ships of Tarshish with the East Wind." (KJV)*

Background

The city of Tyre was a merchant city established on fine wares and luxury trading. It's abundance of goods were transported by impressive cargo ships... the ships of Tarshish. It was a proud city and the people thought they were untouchable. Their god was their wealth, their downfall was their pride and self-sufficiency. They had forgotten about God—*and then came the 'winds of change.' (See Ezekiel 27)*

Prayer of the week

Lord, breathe upon me Your winds of change and let me not despise the seasons You have ordained in my life. Help me to remain humble and dependent on You as my source. Teach me to see each season as a period of new growth, of discipline, of cleansing, of healing and of restoration and refreshing. Deliver me from evil Lord, that I may remain steadfast and dwell in Your house forever. **AMEN**

Thought of the week
The Winds of Change

The Bible talks often of four winds—North, South, East and West. Wind is often used as a metaphor throughout scripture to describe the nature and will of God. God's bidding is often carried out on the currents of the wind and we see examples of this when He brought the plagues of locusts to Egypt via the East wind and restoration via the West Wind.

The North Wind

A cool, powerful wind that brings a tangible freshness. It describes the **presence** of God and it brings deliverance and cleansing.

"Even now men cannot look at the light when it is bright in the skies, when the wind has passed and cleared them. He comes from the north as golden splendour; with God is awesome majesty." **Job 37:21-22**

Acts 2:2 & 4

v2-"and suddenly, there came a sound from heaven, as of a rushing mighty wind, and it filled the whole house where they were sitting..."

v4-"and they were all filled with the Holy Spirit and began to speak in other tongues, as the Spirit gave them utterance."

The East Wind

A hot dry scorching and destructive wind. It describes the **judgment** of God. It reminds us that God is a jealous God and causes us to turn from our sin, from our idolatry and worship Him above all else.

"Though he be fruitful among his brethren, an east wind shall come; the wind of the Lord shall come up from the wilderness. Then his spring shall become dry, and his fountain shall be dried up. He shall plunder the treasury of every desirable prize." **Hosea 13:15**

The West Wind

A very strong and impressive wind. It describes the **restoration** of God and carries with it a new respect and fear of His power and leaves us in awe of his majesty.

"And the Lord turned a very strong west wind, which took the locusts away and blew them into the Red Sea. There remained not one locust in all the territory of Egypt." **Exodus 10:19**

The South Wind

A warm, pleasant, balmy wind. It describes the **refreshing** of the Spirit. It brings soft rain, it makes the plants and the grass grow and flowers to blossom and scatter their perfume abroad. It embraces the knowledge that God is our source, it causes us to 'rise up' and renew our strength in Him.

Job 37:17 *"How thy garments are hot, when he quiets the earth by the south wind."*

Song of Solomon 4:16 *"Awake, O north wind, and come, O south! Blow upon my garden that the spices thereof may flow out. Let my beloved come into his garden and eat his pleasant fruits."*

If we could choose which wind we would like to blow in our direction, I would think most of us would opt for the balmy south wind, the wind that is uplifting and brings calm, peaceful living. As lovely as this sounds and as necessary as times of refreshing are, the reality is that God uses adversity and correction to instil character in us. It is imperative to our growth and in gaining spiritual wisdom and understanding.

It is interesting that of all the winds described in the Bible, the East wind is the most prevalent. It is mentioned at least 21 times. I wonder, does this indicate our predisposition to rebellion or is the judgment and cleansing of the East wind actually an under-valued gift from the treasuries of God that ensures our focus remains true to Him?

Jeremiah 10:13 *"When he utters his voice, there is a multitude of waters in the heavens, and he causes the vapours to ascend from the ends of the earth; he makes lightning for the rain, He brings **the wind out of His treasuries.**"*

Whichever wind God chooses to blow in our direction, we should not despise it but **'count it all joy'**. For each wind serves a unique purpose in our lives and is instrumental in keeping us close to and in tune with His will and it is in the will of God that we find safety, hope and fullness of life.

The winds of God bring life and hope to dead bones

> *"Also, He said he to me, prophesy to the breath* (wind)*, prophesy, son of man, and say to the breath* (wind)*, thus saith the Lord GOD; come from the four winds, O breath, and breathe on these slain, that they may live.*
> **Ezekiel 37:9**

WEEK 14

BE FAITHFUL IN THE SMALL THINGS

Scripture of the week

From: The parable of the Talents – Matthew 25:14-30

Matthew 25:23 "His lord said to him, 'Well done, good and faithful servant, you have been faithful in a few things, I will make you ruler over many things. Enter into the joy of your lord'."

Prayer of the week

Father, in our limited understanding we often feel discontent in our situation and question the timing and outworking of the plan You have for our lives. We get frustrated that we are not yet operating in the fullness of 'the Vision' You have given us. We forget that You see the bigger picture, that there is much training to be undertaken and many tests to be passed before we are ready to finally step into the position You have ordained for us.

In *Your* perfect timing and in *Your* perfect outworking Your will for our lives unfolds. Thank You for Your wisdom. Help us to be patient and faithful in the small, seemingly menial tasks You ask us to do. Empower us to give our best with humility and grace, *right where we are at*. In Jesus name and for Your Glory. **AMEN**

Thought of the week
From little things, big things grow

I know a young man who has both blessed and inspired me beyond measure. He is not famous, he is not rich, he is not highly educated, nor does he hold a glitzy job. What sets this young man apart is *'attitude'*.

His *dream* was to become an electrician and from a very young age he tinkered and dismantled DVD players and other devices... *just to see how they worked.* He dropped out of school in year 10 and a year later returned to school to complete his VCE so that he could attain the grades necessary to enter the electrical trade. He graduated with awards in Robotics, Maths Methods, Physics and Technology. On top of this he completed a pre-apprenticeship and worked part-time within the retail sector.

A pretty gutsy effort! You would like to think that after all that he would have walked straight into an apprenticeship! *Not so...*

At the time he graduated, the bottom had fallen out of the building industry and electrical apprenticeships were almost a non-entity. Rather than let it crush him, he has embraced the opportunities that _**are**_ available to him.

He continues to faithfully apply for positions within his field of choice, all the while determined to give his best right where he is at ***and reaping the rewards of being loyal to his current employer.***

He believes that the door to his dream will one day be opened and refuses to waste his time 'moping about waiting' but rather, he actively and positively contributes value **'right where he is at'.**

A Biblical Parallel

Read: *Genesis 37–Genesis 41*

Joseph had a dream in which one day he would hold a position of authority in the land. In the eyes of his brothers, the dream was above his station. The distance between his current location and the realisation of his dream was a chasm that seemed too wide to cross and when Joseph's brothers threw him in the pit and then sold him to merchants as a slave, he seemed further from the dream than ever before **but**... read the story of Joseph in Genesis and *watch what happens.*

In the midst of uncertainty for the future, allow God to direct your steps

- *"The Lord was with Joseph and he was a successful man ..."* **Genesis 39:2**
- *"But the Lord was with Joseph, and showed him mercy, and gave him favour..."* **Genesis 39.21**

- *"... The Lord was with him; and whatever he did, the Lord made it prosper..."* **Genesis 39:23**

Regardless of the calamity that often surrounded him, Joseph recognised the hand of God on his life and resolved to be faithful *'right there where he was at'*. No, he wasn't yet living *'the dream'* but yes, he _was_ living the will of God for his life. You see Joseph was being groomed for a greater purpose in God but in order to gain the skills and character necessary to meet the responsibility of his 'higher' calling, Joseph needed to humble himself and become a *faithful* servant __where he was at.__

Joseph found favour in every situation he faced through an attitude of diligence, humility, faithfulness, godliness and integrity. With each test passed, God increased His mantle of stewardship until finally after many years, Joseph realised his dream and stood steadfast in the place God had ordained. Joseph could have developed a really bad attitude but instead he opted for a God-Attitude _even_ when wrongly accused and put in prison. In doing so he attained God's best for his life.

So often we forfeit God's best because of pride, discontent and an unwillingness to humble ourselves to the lessons God desires to teach us. We need to learn to be *'faithful in the small things, __right where we are at__'*.

> *"Moreover, it is required in stewards that one be found faithful."*
> **1 Corinthians 4:2**

WEEK 15

CIRCUMCISE YOUR HEART

Scripture of the week

Matthew 5:17-18 *"Do not think that I have come to destroy the Law or the Prophets; I did not come to destroy, but to fulfil. For assuredly, I say to you, till heaven and earth pass away, one jot or one tittle will by no means pass from the Law till all is fulfilled."*

Prayer of the week

Lord, I thank You that through the work of Your salvation we are justified and released from the Old Covenant of the Law and into the New Covenant of Your Love. That through repentance, baptism, obedience and the power of Your Spirit, we allow the circumcision of our hearts and bring our being into line with the heart of the Father and the 'new' commandment, love. Thank You for Your sacrifice, complete and eternal. **AMEN**

Thought of the week
Away with the old

I have been pondering the Old Testament ritual of male circumcision and have realised through my initial research that the subject and its implications are far reaching and more than I could hope to cover in a single devotion, so I will attempt to impart just a little of what I have learnt.

Circumcision of the Jews was performed as an act of obedience by Abraham and his descendants and served as an external and eternal sign of the covenant that God had made with him.

As I read through Old Testament Scriptures and relevant papers on the topic I have come to realise that the act of physical circumcision even in Old Testament times, was meant to be accompanied by a spiritual parallel... circumcision of the heart. Effectively circumcision was an outward sign of an inward reality and was never meant to be merely a physical act.

Deuteronomy 10:16 *"Therefore circumcise the foreskin of your heart, and be stiff-necked no longer."*

Deuteronomy 30:6 *"And the Lord your God will circumcise your heart and the heart of your descendants, to love the Lord your God with all your heart and with all your soul, that you may live."*

Jeremiah 4:4 *"Circumcise yourselves to the Lord and take away the foreskins of your hearts, you men of Judah and inhabitants of Jerusalem, lest My fury come forth like fire, and burn so that no one can quench it, because of the evil of your doings."*

At the ordained time

When my first son was born, I chose not to have him circumcised. It was not the normal procedure at that time and in fact, it was greatly discouraged and deemed unnecessary.

At the age of nearly 2 my son had to be circumcised for medical reasons. It was the most hideous of operations I have ever encountered. The immense pain and fear on his face when the anaesthetic wore off, the way in which he extended and stiffened his limbs and the endless and unceasing cries of excruciating pain whenever I changed his nappy will be forever imprinted on my brain.

After much agonising, research and soul searching we decided to have our second son circumcised at birth, actually at exactly eight days after birth. I had to seek out a Jewish doctor well in advance who warned me that if I did not attend to the procedure *at the ordained time* that he would not perform it afterwards.

I was present for the operation which was performed in the procedure room of what seemed very much like a GP's office. The contrast to the circumcision of my elder son was astounding. It took all of a few minutes in total and there was little or no blood, no anaesthetic, no stitches and no bandages. He cried for only a few minutes and then not again afterwards. The healing was so much faster and with much less discomfort and pain. In fact, he slept soundly in the car all the way home, fed and nestled contentedly that night and never really cried even when I cleaned him during bathing and nappy changing.

The Lesson learned...

When we allow God to circumcise our hearts—*at His appointed time*, the healing is faster and the pain less onerous. The longer we leave the act of circumcision of our hearts, the greater the pain and the struggles we must suffer. We will require spiritual stitches and bandages and the process will inevitably leave us with wounds that are slow to heal and which render us ineffective until such time as sufficient healing has taken place. I personally wish I had learned this lesson sooner.

Medicine confirms the wisdom of God

There was wisdom in God's instruction that a child should be circumcised on the eight day, even if that day fell on the Sabbath.

In 1935 a Professor by the name of H. Dam discovered what God already knew, that Vitamin K (produced by bacteria in the intestinal tract) was responsible for the production (by the liver) of Prothrombin, an element which when coupled with Vitamin K caused 'blood coagulation'. These elements are not generally present in sufficient quantities until days 5-7 after birth. On the eighth day however, the levels of Vitamin K and Prothrombin are at their peak and is in fact the only day in a male's life in which the levels are elevated above one hundred percent of normal. Therefore the 8th day is the day where blood coagulation is at its best–the *perfect* day for surgery.[1]

But what about the here and now?

Jesus said…"*Do not think that I have come to destroy the Law or the Prophets; I did not come to destroy, but to fulfil. For assuredly, I say to you, till heaven and earth pass away, one jot or one tittle will by no means pass from the Law till all is fulfilled." **Matthew 5:17-18***

During His life and by His death and resurrection, Christ fulfilled <u>all</u> the requirements of the law. He was the perfect sin sacrifice because He was blameless, perfect and without sin, *even* after having been tempted. He brought us into a new covenant not based on rules and rituals but based on a higher spiritual covenant, love… and this love covenant actually <u>*magnifies the intent*</u> of the original Law commandments passed to Moses from God the Father.

In the Old Testament the law addressed the act of murder as a physical act but in the New Testament that same act is addressed at a *higher spiritual level.* ***1 John 3:15*** *"Whoever hates his brother is a murderer, and you know that no murderer has eternal life abiding in him."*

God's eternal principles of the law were not made void but rather fully revealed at Calvary. The requirement for continued sacrifice however was <u>*paid in full*</u>, *once and for all eternity* and this perfect justification is accessible to those who believe by faith. No longer are we required by law to circumcise our flesh but to be obedient to the 'spirit' or 'intent' of the law which reflects the heart of God.

WEEK 16

THE POWER SOURCE

Scripture of the week

Ephesians 3:20 "*Now to Him who is able to do exceedingly abundantly above all that we ask or think, according to the power that works in us.*"

Prayer of the week

Lord, during Your ministry on earth You modelled and provided perfect examples of how we should live our lives and the attitudes we should adopt. Instil in me a desire to seek out and imitate those examples. Help me to relinquish my will to that of Your Spirit that I might walk in the fullness of Your power. **AMEN**

Thought of the week
The Power Source

It is a standing joke at work when people come into my office that they are entering the '*sauna*'. It doesn't matter how hot it is, my hands and feet are always cold. It could be 35 degrees Celsius outside and you will find me sitting behind my desk tapping away at the keyboard with the door closed and the heater pointed directly at my feet. If I can't get semi-warm, I cannot get my fingers to work.

Whilst many people complain of high blood pressure, I have the opposite issue, consistently low blood pressure and because I sit at a desk all day with very little gross motor movement, the blood makes a bee-line for my brain (in order to keep that functioning) and flows even slower to my feet and hands. As a result my extremities are always cold, in fact verging on 'freezing'.

The answer to my problem is very simple, I need to exercise more. I need to get my heart pumping and *unleash the power* that allows my blood to circulate more effectively.

A bit about blood

Blood is considered the ***life source*** of our physical bodies. It is the carrier of nutrients, of hormones and of oxygen. It has the important function of removing toxic waste products which, if left unchecked, would build up and effectively poison us. It clots when we bleed and has a significant role in the subsequent healing process. The blood regulates our fluid volumes, our pH levels and our body temperature and it carries the white blood cells and antibodies that help us fight infection. In essence it is the ***active ingredient*** responsible for maintaining bodily health and vitality.

The blood provides us with the ***power*** to effectively live a physical human life but if we neglect to take the necessary steps to ensure that it is able to circulate freely within us then we end up functioning below capacity or as in my case, living with cold extremities.

Hmm... I can feel an analogy developing!

The Ministry of the Person of the Holy Spirit

Jesus was speaking to His Disciples in the book of Acts, *"... He commanded them not to depart from Jerusalem but to wait for the Promise of the Father which, He said you have heard from Me; for John truly baptised with water, but you shall be baptized with the Holy Spirit not many days from now." **Acts 1:4-5***

*"But you shall receive **power** when the Holy Spirit has come upon you; and you shall be witnesses to me in Jerusalem, and in all Judea and Samaria and to the end of the earth." **Acts 1:8***

What Jesus was saying to the Disciples was that when they received the promise of the Baptism in the Holy Spirit they would, through Him (the Holy Spirit) receive the **power** to continue the work of His (Jesus) Ministry. The **power** to live the Christian life with victory. *The **power** to finish the race <u>triumphantly</u>!*

Tapping into the source...

Just as blood provides life to our bodies, the Spirit provides life to our whole person.

When we adopt healthy eating habits and exercise we release the blood to do its work, to circulate and permeate our physical bodies so that we can function at optimum physical levels. *But even greater than this...* when we feast on <u>healthy spiritual food</u> and <u>exercise our free will</u> by yielding it to that of the Spirit, we ***allow*** Him to circulate, empower and permeate our lives. In doing this, <u>*every aspect of our person*</u> is able to function at optimum levels and it is in the yielding of our lives to His leading that the glory of His power is revealed. *Relinquishing our will to that of the Holy Spirit is an* <u>*active choice.*</u>

The Example of Jesus...

Jesus was:
- ***Filled*** *with the Holy Spirit* ***(Luke 1:15)***;
- ***Led*** *by the Holy Spirit* ***(Luke 4:1 & 14)***; and
- ***Empowered*** *by the Holy Spirit* ***(Matthew 12:28)***

Food for thought

If Jesus, the beloved Son of God deemed it crucial to submit His will to the leading of the Holy Spirit in every aspect of His life how much more so should we submit to the Holy Spirits leading?

> *"The Spirit of the Lord is upon me, because he has anointed me to preach the gospel to the poor; He has sent me to heal the broken-hearted, to preach deliverance to the captives, and recovering of sight to the blind, to set at liberty them that are oppressed, to preach the acceptable year of the Lord."*
> ***Luke 4:18-19***

WEEK 17

'ALIEN' CORRESPONDENCE!

Scripture of the week

John 17:14-16 "*I have given them Your Word; and the world has hated them because they are not of the world, just as I am not of the world. I do not pray that You should take them out of the world, but that You should keep them from the evil one. They are <u>not of the world</u>, just as I am not of the world.*" (Part of Jesus' prayer for the Disciples).

Prayer of the week

Father, before I was born You *knew* me. Before I was born You *set me apart*. Your call was on my life before it even began and I thank You that You are able to complete the good work You have begun in me. I thank You that You have never given up on me, even when I have turned my back on You. Forgive me Lord; create in me a new heart, a heart of flesh and not of wood. A heart that would burn not for things that are carnal but for things that bring spiritual life and glory to Your name. Keep me from the evil one. In Jesus name. **AMEN**

Thought of the week
'Alien' Correspondence

I was having a D&M (deep and meaningful) with a girlfriend. We have been friends for over 20 years and the conversations are easy and uninhibited. She has seen the worst and the best of me and loves me in spite of it. I have recently moved in with her and we were discussing how well I was settling in and I had to be honest... *I'm not*. We conversed back and forth for some time exploring the reasons why it was difficult for me to feel like here (or anywhere else for that matter) was 'home' and I ended up going to bed not really any wiser on the subject.

A little background...

In my life I have shifted over 50 times and as a child went to 13 different schools (that I can remember anyway). As a result I have never bothered to set down roots, I can be socially awkward and I can often come across as 'stand-offish'. I have a tendency to be insular and as a result I have very few 'close friends'. For most of my life I have had this pervading sense that *I do not fit or belong* and nothing I did seemed to quench that gap in my life. So, I went to bed that night no closer to understanding why I feel the way I do... **I woke up to a revelation.**

I realised that the reason I don't feel I belong here is because *actually **I don't***. Realistically I will probably <u>never</u> feel truly 'home' until I either die or Jesus comes back and I am changed in a *"twinkling of an eye"* at the final trumpet sound. **(see 1 Corinthians 15:52).** *Ooh, how exciting is that!*

John 17:14-16 indicates that while we are called to be *in* the world we are not actually *of* the world... so, it stands to reason that I would feel the *'alien'* way I do.

*"Beloved, I beg you as **sojourners,*** (temporary residents/aliens/foreigners) *and **pilgrims,*** (one who embarks on a sacred quest as an act of devotion) *abstain from fleshly lusts which war against the soul." **1 Peter 2:11***

The second part of that revelation is that **<u>I am ok with it</u>**. Time is short and not a second can be wasted on feeling sorry for myself. The reality is <u>I am not my own</u>, I was brought at a price *(see **1 Corinthians 6:20**)* and as such in everything I am and everything I do I am compelled to be Christ focused. So, until such time as I go to be with my Father, all of my energy and all of my time has to have a kingdom focus because, *time is short* and people are dying without ever having heard the gospel. Yes, I might be tired here for a short time but, in contrast, I will be eternally refreshed when I get to go home.

I have another good friend who is *so* dedicated and focused towards the call of God on his life that everything else fades into insignificance. For the first time in my life I really *'get that'*, I understand it. <u>*I feel the urgency of it.*</u>

So, while I have breath, I will bring my body and my mind into submission and ignore these self-focused feelings of being tired and not really belonging anywhere, for these will be fully satisfied in time. In the interim I will do what I can to ensure this body stays healthy enough to do the work and 'keep pressing forward'.

1 Corinthians 9:24–27 *(NIV).*

- *v24)* *"Do you not know that in a race all the runners run, but only one gets the prize?* **Run in such a way as to get the prize.***"*
- *v25)* *"Everyone who competes in the games goes into strict training. They do it to get a crown that will not last;* **but we do it to get a crown that will last forever.***"*
- *v26)* *"Therefore* **I do not run like a man running aimlessly***; I do not fight like a man beating the air."*
- *v27)* *"No,* **I beat my body and make it my slave** *so that after I have preached to others, I myself will not be disqualified for the prize."*

A testimonial side note: God can turn the bad around and use it for good.

Satan meant to use the insecurity of my life to crush and to harm me <u>but</u> God has taken that same experience and used it to build strength in me. Very few people could have sustained being uprooted as many times as I have but what had the potential to cripple me, God has used to prepare me. My ability to pick up, leave everything behind and relocate, I now view as a gift... a unique gift that will assist me to walk in the call of God on my life.

Jeremiah 1:5 *"Before I formed you in the womb I knew you; before you were born I sanctified you; and I ordained you a prophet to the nations."*

The following is a verse and chorus of a song I wrote some years ago... and which I found during my recent move. It reminds me that God *knew me before I was formed* and that His hand has been on my life for my <u>whole</u> life, and even when I chose not to heed His call, He continued to woo me with His song.

You sang me a love song...

I can't believe I've come this far as I look back on my years
the pain and hurt, abuse and fear
the torment without tears.

But now I know these things have made me
who I am today and Lord I want to thank You
for each step of the way.

Because
You sang me a love song
a voice from the grave
a beautiful love song
of mercy and grace.

Felicity Eagan

"For I know the thoughts that I think
toward you, says the Lord,
thoughts of peace and not of evil, to
give you a future and a hope."
Jeremiah 29:11

WEEK 18

TEST AND MEASURE

Scripture of the week

2 Timothy 2:15 *"Be diligent to present yourself approved to God; a worker who does not need to be ashamed, rightly dividing the word of truth."*

Prayer of the week

Father, Your word is a lamp unto my feet and a light unto my path... it is the Word of Life; it does not return void and; it accomplishes that which You desire to be accomplished. It is through the hearing of Your Word that faith is established in my heart and Your Word is integral to the very foundation of my faith. Help me not to trivialise the importance of Your Word and the power contained therein. For when I know Your Word I am immersed in Your Truth and Your Truth sets me free. **AMEN**

Thought of the week

Test and measure

As I was writing the *'Femail Encourager'* one evening, I went to insert a 'verse' that I felt was relevant to the topic. At the last moment I thought I should probably reference that verse. I am so glad I did. Somewhere in my Christian walk I had been told that it says in the Bible *'be in the world, not of the world'* and being a young Christian, I have just adopted and accepted this as truth.

Well! You can imagine my surprise when after having searched my concordances and 'Googled' extensively I could NOT find such a verse. Whilst the concept behind this phrase can be derived from scripture *(namely John 17:14-16)*, the words that I had thought were scripture actually were NOT.

This simple error rocked me to the core. I have frequently quoted this phrase to others truly believing it to be a verse in the Bible. So I am left wondering how many other inaccurate beliefs form part of the foundation of my faith?

Question, validate, question, validate, question, question, question...

Philippians 2:12 "Therefore, my beloved, as you have always obeyed, not as in my presence only, but now much more in my absence, work out your own salvation with fear and trembling."

Concepts can be transferred from person to person but spiritual truths must be discerned *(1 Corinthians 2:14)*. Discernment comes from the Holy Spirit in you and the Sword (weapon) of the Spirit- THE WORD OF GOD. So, what I am saying is it is important that you do not blindly accept anything that I (or anyone else), says without questioning its validity and testing it against the Word of God.

TEACHERS are accountable before God for what they teach but **YOU** are accountable before God for what you believe.

A case of ignorance

I obtained my licence in Queensland and when visiting another State I got pulled over by the police whilst still on my Probationary licence. In Queensland it was not a requirement to display 'P' plates and so I was not aware I was required to display them when driving here. As a result I got fined and had to appear in court.

I distinctly remember the judge saying to me these words... *"Ignorance is <u>no excuse</u> for the law".*

So it is with your faith... *ignorance is <u>no excuse</u>.* The book outlining the truth is available to you (The Bible) but to benefit from its wisdom you need to immerse yourself in it and understand it. Had I have bothered to read the book telling me the local rules for wearing 'P' plates I might have avoided a court appearance and hefty fine.

The Importance of Immersing Yourself in the Word

It will help you to discern between Truth and lies...*"Beware lest anyone cheat you through philosophy and empty deceit, according to the tradition of men, according to the basic principles of the world, and not according to Christ."* **Colossians 2:8**

Spiritual discernment is so important and Jesus warns about blindly accepting false doctrines in **Matthew 15:13-14** *"But He answered and said, every plant which My heavenly Father has not planted will be uprooted. Let them alone. They are blind leaders of the blind. And if the blind leads the blind, both will fall into a ditch."* (Referring to the teaching of the Pharisees).

It is the weapon by which we thwart spiritual attack. The Word of God is the Sword of the Spirit, it is the weapon used to cut down the enemy. When we are immersed in the Word, we fight with the Sword of the King, forged from unbreakable, hardened steel. But when our Biblical understanding is poor we fight with little more than a rusty pocket knife, ineffective and easily overcome by the weapons of the enemy.

It is the benchmark for the renewing our minds...
The Word is the living water that brings victory and abundant life. *"And do not be conformed to this world, but be transformed by the renewing of your mind, that you may prove what is that good and acceptable and perfect will of God."* **Romans 12:2**

A healthy perspective

Shortly after receiving her copy of the *'Femail Encourager'*, one of the ladies on my mailing list contacted me to ask me *'where I had got my information'*. PRAISE GOD!

Well, I can say that now but I have to admit that at the time, my initial reaction was to cringe and think

"Oh boy here we go". I truly had a personal struggle with being challenged. However, what developed was not a confrontation but instead, a sincere questioning of a concept that was unfamiliar to her. She was merely trying to understand and discern for herself whether what I had written had Biblical foundation. And so she asked where I had derived my research so that she could examine it for herself. Her heart wasn't to criticise but to seek understanding.

... to work out her salvation with fear and trembling.
... to be accountable for her own belief and not accept my words blindly.

I was blessed... so, so blessed! Still blessed writing about it!

I truly believe that God called me to write these devotions and in accepting the call, I am fully aware of the mantle of responsibility that comes with it. I labour over each one and pray that the words I impart will be anointed and based in Truth.

But having said this, I am human and at times I am going to get it wrong. So please, I implore you... always, always, always read what I write with a discerning spirit and test it against the Truth of God's Word. Never accept my words or the teaching of others merely at face value but question and research and pray through them for yourself.

If it doesn't sit right with you, don't just accept it, question, explore and research. If it doesn't line up with what you know about God from His Word then either reject it or mark it for further examination.

> *"Beloved, do not believe every spirit, but test*
> *the spirits, whether they are of God;*
> *because many false prophets have gone out into the world."*
> **1 John 4:1**

WEEK 19

STRAWBERRY PANACOTTA!

Scripture of the week

Luke 11:34 *"The lamp of the body is the eye. Therefore when your eye is good, your whole body also is full of light. But when your eye is bad, your body is also full of darkness."*

Prayer of the week

Lord, help me to discern what is holy in a world so desensitised to sin that it is accepted as normal. Instil in me the desire to fill my mind and meditate on things that are noble and good and pure. Convict me when I turn my eyes away from You and gaze upon things that lead to temptation that I might remain pure and sanctified. In Jesus name. **AMEN**

Thought of the week
Watch your diet!

What you see (and hear) feeds the soul... *good and bad alike.*

Quote:
"Whatever captures their eyes and ears will also capture their minds and hearts."
(Author Unknown)

Danger! Strawberry Panacotta!

I opened the door and there it was... *strawberry panacotta!* My eyes beheld the glorious sight and as my eyes feasted my taste buds began to salivate with anticipation. I closed the door s-l-o-w-l-y but it was too late. *The seed had been sown* and as my mind's eye kept replaying that tantalising vision the seed swelled and expanded and took root until finally it consumed me and I gave in to the lust of my desire, *all 1050 kilojoules of it.*

You are what you eat

I have recently put on about 7kgs (doctor's orders) and Oh the joy of being able to eat unchecked! The problem is I have now hit my ideal weight and need to curb any further weight gain, *easier said than done*!

After I had my children I struggled to lose the weight I gained during pregnancy. I tried and failed time and time again and found myself gorging biscuits and cakes and all things bad! The more sugar and fat I consumed, the more I wanted. I would buy things determined not to touch them but I knew they were there, lurking in the cupboards... tempting me to have *just ONE... then TWO* and then **THE WHOLE PACKET!** Each time I opened the door, there they were mocking me and with each viewing my resolve lessened and without fail I caved and gave in, only to feel shame at my lack of self-control.

Out of sight out of mind

One day I found the key to success... *remove the temptation from sight.* Don't buy them in the first place! If they are not in the house my eye does not kick-start the internal battle of desire and deprivation. By removing the source of the temptation from my view, I was able to stick to a healthy diet that enabled a healthy body. If I saw it, I wanted it and the wanting eventually consumed me... *the answer was not to see it in the first place.*

No one is immune

Not even King David, the man after God's own heart *(Acts 13:22).* King David had sent his men to battle and was lounging around. In his idleness, his eyes wandered to the quarters of a neighbouring house and to a beautiful woman, Bathsheba, the wife of another man. And so the wandering eye of King David set in motion a lust of the flesh that would cause him to sin not once, but several times in an attempt to cover his wrong doing.

David not only committed adultery but he lied in order to try and cover Bathsheba's pregnancy. When his lie failed, he had her husband Uriah murdered. King David 'saw', he became 'consumed with lust' and he 'gave in to temptation'. He fed his mind with that which was unwholesome and paid a terrible price for it. *(see 2 Samuel: Chapters 11 and 12)*

Job got it right when he said: *"I made a covenant with my eyes not to look lustfully at a girl." **Job 31:1** (NIV).* He chose not to sin against his own body or against God and recognised that the mere act of looking would place him on the road to sin.

Do not set your eyes on anything that is worthless
(based on Psalm 101:3)

The media has desensitised us to such a point that we casually feed our minds with music and movies that are saturated with sex, murder, adultery, pornography, witchcraft and think nothing of it. I have found myself challenged on a number of occasions lately about the trash I flippantly allow to fill my mind without a second thought. Would I be watching this if Jesus was sitting beside me? And then I realise, *He is!*

Philippians 4:8 *"...whatever things are true, whatever things are noble, whatever things are just, whatever things are lovely, whatever things are of good report, if there is any virtue and if there is anything praiseworthy, meditate on these things."*

"Turn your eyes upon Jesus
Look full in His wonderful face
and the things on earth will grow strangely dim
in the light of His glory and grace"
(Extract from the Hymn – Turn
Your Eyes Upon Jesus)

WEEK 20

STARING AT THE SAND DUNES

Scripture of the week

2 Corinthians 12:9a *"And He said to me, 'My grace is sufficient for you, for My strength is made perfect in weakness...'"*

Prayer of the week

Lord, teach me to bring everything to You in prayer and supplication that I might be anxious for nothing. Let Your peace–the peace that passes all understanding, guard my heart and mind. In Jesus name. **AMEN** *(see Philippians 4:6-7)*

Thought of the week
Staring at the sand dunes

What do you do when your soul is dry and you can't feel the presence of the Spirit of God?... *You hold on to the promise that He will never leave you or forsake you.*

How do you keep pressing forward when the honeymoon is over and you are surrounded by hard work requiring discipline and somewhere along the way you have become lost in the sandstorm of life?... *You direct your gaze towards* the cross and humbly acknowledge that it is "**not by might nor by power but by His Spirit**" *(Zechariah 4:6)* that you will endure the desert times.

... AND YOU SING

You bring the *'sacrifice of praise' (Hebrews 13:15)*. You worship even when your soul cries out with barrenness and your throat is parched and raspy. SACRIFICE means to suffer a loss or...*"I choose to die to self and offer praise to God in spite of how I feel"*. It's easy to praise when everything is going well—a lot harder when life keeps throwing mud in your face!

Quote:
"The loudest praise comes very often from the ones who are passing through hardships."
(Watchman Nee)

... AND YOU PRAY

Even when after the praying you feel no different, clinging to that mustard seed of faith and believing with confidence that He hears your prayers for no other reason than *He said so...*

Daniel 10:12-13 "Do not fear Daniel for from that first day that you set your heart to understand and to humble yourself before your God, your words were heard; and I have come because of your words. But the prince of the kingdom of Persia withstood me twenty one days; and behold, Michael, one of the chief princes, came to help me, for I had been left alone there with the kings of Persia."

God sent his angel, the first day of Daniel's prayer. God heard his prayer and he responded to the call. But we fight not against *'flesh and blood'* but against *'principalities and powers' (**Ephesians 6:12**)* and the battle going on in the Spiritual realm delayed the Angel of the Lord and with him the answer to Daniel's prayer.

Do not fear or be dismayed

So my encouragement to you is *'hang in there'*. When you are staring at the sandstorm, know that it will pass. Keep looking forward and upward even when you think that God has not heard your prayer, when you feel alone and your soul feels empty remember... He promises to never leave you or forsake you—so regardless of what you see or feel, determine to walk by *'faith'* and not by *'sight'*. *(**2 Corinthians 5:7**)*

> *"And the Lord, He is the One who goes*
> *before you. He will be with you,*
> *He will not leave you nor forsake you;*
> *do not fear or be dismayed."*
> **Deuteronomy 31:8**

WEEK 21

SO MUCH MORE

Scripture of the week

Matthew 7:11 *"If you then, being evil, know how to give good gifts to your children HOW MUCH MORE will your Father who is in heaven give good things to those who ask Him?"* (Emphasis mine).

Prayer of the week

Mighty God! Thank You for the truths set out in Your Word. Thank You that You are able to achieve great things through us even though we are weak. Empower us to ask for and embrace those opportunities You present to us that we might rise to the call and take a step of faith and be the vessel You have chosen to use for the extension of Your kingdom. Knowing Lord, that as we are faithful in the small things, you will continue to extend us—precept, upon precept, upon precept. **AMEN**

Thought of the week
So much more

Matthew 7:7-11 *"Ask, and it will be given to you; seek, and you will find; knock, and it will be opened to you. For everyone who asks receives and he who seeks finds and to him who knocks, it will be opened. O what man is there among* *you who, if his son asks for bread, will give him a stone? Or if he asks for a fish, will he give him a serpent? If you then, being evil, know how to give good gifts to your children how much more will your Father who is in heaven give good things to those who ask Him?"*

If you could dream and have everything you wanted in life what would that be?

Would your list include:

- To be financially free
- Well educated children
- A great job
- A new car
- A husband
- To own your own home
- More friends
- Good health
- A stress free life?

... you get the general idea.

None of these things are sinful or wrong and when we seek God for these, He hears our prayers and is faithful in providing those things that we need. But God is saying that He has SO MUCH MORE for us than just the immediate and obvious needs, and that often we limit the full outworking of what He wants for our lives because we fail to ask for more.

He wants SO MUCH MORE for our lives! He has SO MUCH MORE to give us, if only we would divert our focus from a bread and fish mentality to *"Father, let Your kingdom come through me"*.

Our grandest dreams fall so far short of what God wants for our lives... so far short of what He wants to do in us and through us. Abraham had a dream for a son but God had a plan SO MUCH BIGGER. God's plan for Abraham was to be the father of a nation... a plan far beyond Abraham's wildest dreams and limited understanding.

1 Corinthians 1:26-28 *"For you see your calling, brethren, that not many wise according to the flesh, not many mighty, not many noble, are called. But God has chosen the foolish things of the world to put to shame the wise, and God has chosen the weak things of the world to put to shame the things which are mighty; and the base* (insignificant or lowly) *things of the world and the things which are despised God has chosen, and the things which are not, to bring to nothing the things that are, that no flesh should glory in his presence."*

He desires to outwork His kingdom through us and yet so often we settle for 'bread and fish' prayers because we think:

- I'm not worthy
- I'm too old
- I'm too young
- I'm too sick

- I'm too uneducated
- I'm too shy
- I'm not good enough
- I don't have the skills

... sound familiar?

If you fit into any of the categories above then guess what, YOU ARE THE PERFECT CANDIDATE to do great things for God because His strength is made perfect in your weakness... that *"the flesh should not glory but God's kingdom should glory"*.

As believers we are called to have a higher vision above and beyond that of the world, yet sometimes in our limited perception we hold back the full purpose of what God has for us because:

- We fail to **ASK** beyond bread and fish.
- We fail to **SEEK** out opportunities to show the love of Christ which sets us apart from the world.
- We fail to **KNOCK** or take that first step of faith by 'moving' in the direction God points—no matter how small.

Matthew 6:9-11 *"In this manner, therefore, pray: Our Father in heaven, hallowed be Your name. Your kingdom come, Your will be done on earth as it is in heaven. Give us this day our daily bread."*

For many of us our priorities are upside down. Jesus teaches us the order in which we should pray yet so often our prayers head down the track of ...*"Lord, Give us our 'long list of daily bread and fish requests' and "oh yeah"... Your kingdom come!"*

"In this manner, therefore, pray:"

Step 1–(Praise and Worship - God Focus)-*"Our Father in Heaven Hallowed be YOUR name."*

Step 2–(Kingdom Focus)-*YOUR kingdom come, Your will be done on earth as it is in heaven."*

Step 3–(Bread and Fish)-*"Give us this day our daily bread."*

God knows your needs, he knows your desires *(see Matthew 6:31-33).* Our bread and fish lists are so insignificant by comparison to HOW MUCH MORE He has for your life. ASK God for something beyond what you can see and believe that through Christ you are worthy and capable of achieving great things for the glory of His Kingdom.

SEEK God for opportunities to use the gifts He has given you... to show love beyond worldly understanding and then KNOCK or TAKE ACTION. It is not enough to identify opportunities you must *take a step of faith.*

Exodus 14:15-16 *"And the Lord said to Moses, "Why do you cry to Me? Tell the children of Israel to GO FORWARD"* (Move! Take Action), *but lift up your rod and stretch out your hand over the sea and divide it. And the children of Israel shall go on dry ground through the midst of the sea."* (Emphasis mine).

Just like Moses, God is waiting for YOU to take action! And as you walk in obedience in the direction that He points, He will show up and His power and glory will be poured out upon you, enabling YOU to do things far greater than you could have ever imagined possible.

A woman of action

I had the privilege of knowing a woman who did great things for God. In the natural this woman would not have been high up on the world's list of the *'most likely to succeed'*, she was not well educated, she was riddled with ill health yet continued to preach until the day she died at age 74. She had a gift... the gift of being willing to move in whatever direction God pointed, without question, without reservation, totally sold out for Jesus.

For many years she was a missionary to many different nations and in her latter years she worked tirelessly as an International Ambassador for Christ. She was recognised by her peers and this uneducated woman was awarded an Honorary Doctorate for her contribution to world missions.

The point I am trying to make is that she was just an ordinary woman (no different from you or I) who was totally sold out for Jesus and willing to follow Him in whichever direction He lead. She would drive me nuts because she would spill sugar on the bench every time she made a cup of tea and neglect to clean it up, but this woman lead more people to Jesus than anyone I have ever known. Her priority was not to clean up sugar but to show the love of Jesus to the lost. Her focus was not on bread and fish but on seeing God's kingdom come.

I once said to her *"You can't help yourself can you?"* and her response was *"tell me, if you suddenly found a cure for cancer what would you do?"* My reply, *"tell people with cancer."* *"Exactly!"* she said. She would wake every morning and pray (ask) for a 'divine appointment' and she would seek expectantly for the opportunities that God presented to her and then act on every opportunity without any doubt that God would honour her faith. In 2013 this woman went home to be with Jesus... I praise God for her life and for her kingdom focus and I rejoice that when she stands before her God I know that she will hear those words *"well done good and faithful servant—come forward and receive your crown."*

So... if you're sitting there tonight reading this and knowing in your heart that there must be more than just bread and fish... *shift your focus*! Ask for opportunities to be used as a vessel through which He will extend His kingdom and when those opportunities are presented to you, then TAKE ACTION. You will never be 100% sure of all the details but if you take that step of faith in the direction He points and walk through the doors as He opens them He will show up and through YOU He will do great things for the glory of His kingdom.

> *"Now when the multitudes saw it, they marvelled*
> *and glorified God, who had given such power to men."*
> **Matthew 9:8**

WEEK 22

FOR THE LOVE OF FLY BUYS

Scripture of the week

Revelation 22:12 *"And behold I am coming quickly, and My reward is with Me, to give to everyone according to his work."*

Prayer of the week

Lord, teach me <u>Your</u> ways. **AMEN**

Thought of the week
For the love of Fly Buys

If you look in the average woman's purse what will you find? *Go on! Have a peak in yours*!

Well I am embarrassed to say that mine is filled to the brim with member rewards cards, 25 of them actually! Reward cards for coffee, grocery rewards cards, retail stores, entertainment venues, insurance loyalty program and even a frequent blood donor card, and this is all in the purse of someone who hates shopping!

As a society we love rewards! It's in our make-up.
The Bible talks about rewards in the form of heavenly crowns... awarded to believers for dedication and service to God performed whilst alive on this earth. On the day

of judgement we will receive a crown or several crowns according to our passion and allegiance to the gospel, and according to our dedication and pursuit of good works, inspired by God and kingdom focused.

Before I go on I want to make it clear that good works will not get you into Heaven. Salvation and good works are completely separate. The Bible clearly tells us that salvation cannot be earned, that it is a free gift and we can ONLY be saved by grace through faith in Jesus Christ. It is important that I clarify this so that there is no confusion or misunderstanding in what I am writing.

Ephesians 2:8-9 *"For by grace have been saved through faith, and that not of yourselves; it is the gift of God, not of works, lest any man should boast."*

If you confess your sin, turn from your sinful ways and believe in your heart by faith that the Lord Jesus Christ died, was buried and rose again in your place. Then you are SAVED! Full stop! Period! If at the point of confession you had died whilst never having ever done a single good work you would have been assured of a place in Heaven. YOU WERE 100% saved by GRACE.

Romans 10:9 *"That if you confess with your mouth the Lord Jesus and believe in your heart that God has raised him from the dead, you will be saved."*

The Bible says that we were created for good works
Ephesians 2:10 *"For we are His workmanship, created in Christ Jesus for good works, which God prepared beforehand, that we should walk in them."*

When we sign up for a loyalty program we become an irrefutable member, but it is only when we actively participate in that program that we build up credits that can later be exchanged for rewards.

Heavenly rewards—5 crowns

As I worked my way through the 5 heavenly crowns listed in the Bible it became evident to me that it is God's intention to reward us for our faithfulness to His call and for our willingness to serve above and beyond His gift of salvation. His desire is for us to actively participate in His heavenly rewards program and extend His kingdom here on earth.

1. <u>The Imperishable Crown</u>
(Also known as the "Victors Crown" or the "Incorruptible Crown")
1 Corinthians 9:24-25 *"Do you not know that those who run in a race all run, but one receives the prize? Run in such a way that you may obtain it. And everyone who competes for the prize is temperate* (exercises self-control) *in all things. Now they do it to obtain a perishable crown but we for an imperishable crown."*

The Imperishable crown is awarded to those who run the race to completion, those who just like an elite athlete exercise strict self-control and strive to give their 'everything' in order to win the prize. They sacrifice themselves and often what is seen as *'the good things of this world'* for the higher calling of God.

2. <u>The Crown of Rejoicing</u>

1 Thessalonians 2:19-20 *"For what is our hope, or joy, or crown of rejoicing? Is it not even you in the presence of our Lord Jesus Christ at His coming? For you are our glory and joy."*

This crown is given to those who win souls for Christ, Christians so moved by compassion for those whose don't know Christ that their life's work is one of evangelism. They are so motivated to reach as many people for Christ as possible that they cannot help but spread the 'good news' of Christ to whoever they encounter despite the risks, despite feeling challenged, opposed and intimidated. They are not ashamed of the gospel for they know that it is the power of God unto salvation.

3. <u>The Crown of Life</u>

(Also known as the "Martyrs Crown")

James 1:12 *"Blessed is the man who endures temptation; for when he has been proved, he will receive the crown of life which the Lord has promised to those who love Him."*

This is the crown for those who suffer trials and tribulations for the sake of the kingdom, for those whose faith has been tested and who have remained steadfast and true, *even unto death.*

4. <u>The Crown of Righteousness</u>

2 Timothy 4:8 *"Finally, there is laid up for me the crown of righteousness, which the Lord, the righteous Judge, will give to me on that Day, and not to me only but also to all who have loved his appearing."*

At first I struggled to understand what the phrase *'who have loved his appearing'* meant and couldn't find any references that explained it well but then I came across an explanation by **William MacDonald** who wrote the devotional *'One Day at a Time'*. He described it like this... *"To love His appearing means to live in the light of His coming, to behave as if He were coming today. Thus, to love His appearing means to live in moral purity."* This crown is for those who have lived a life of righteousness, a life pleasing and honouring to the Lord, a life in which you would be pleased for the Lord to find you living.

5. <u>The Crown of Glory</u>

(Also known as the "Elders Crown")

1 Peter 5:1-4 *"The elders who are among you I exhort, I who am a fellow elder and a witness of the sufferings of Christ, and also a partaker of the glory that will be revealed: Shepherd the flock of God which is among you, serving as overseers, not by constraint but willingly, not for dishonest gain but eagerly; nor as being lords over those entrusted to you, but being examples to the flock; and when the Chief Shepherd appears, you will receive the crown of glory that does not fade away".*

The crown is for the Pastors, the Preachers, the Teachers, the Shepherds; for those who minister eagerly and who faithfully feed the flock; for those who devotedly teach the word of God to others; for those whose motivation is to nurture the sheep entrusted to their care, that each one might rise up and realise their full potential in God. For those willing to serve and suffer great personal sacrifice for the glory of the Father and for the love of His flock.

Now is the time

It is never too late to undertake good works for the Lord. He created you for just that purpose and when you walk in the fullness of that which God created you for then it is there that you will find fulfilment and purpose, beyond the perishable rewards of this world. God inspired good works have eternal value that He promises to reward with heavenly crowns.

"...looking unto Jesus, the author and
finisher of our faith, who for
the joy that was set before Him endured
the cross, despising the shame,
and has sat down at the right hand of the throne of God."
Hebrews 12:2

WEEK 23

HEDGE ME LORD

Scripture of the week

John 15:1-2 *"I am the Vine, and My Father is the Vinedresser. Every branch in Me that does not bear fruit He takes away; and every branch that bears fruit He prunes, that it may bear more fruit."*

Prayer of the week

Father, thank You for the gift of Your Word. The two-edged sword that is capable of cutting through my hardest attitudes, thoughts and misconceptions. Lord I am willing to allow Your pruning, knowing that Your intention for my life is good and motivated by the loving care of the Vinedresser. I acknowledge that it is through the trials and tribulations of my life and through the testing of my faith that I will gain perseverance and Christ-like character and with this knowledge planted deep in my heart I will joy in You my Saviour and Lord. **AMEN**

Thought of the week
Hedge me Lord

I am a bit of a gardener and one of my greatest loves is a neatly sculptured hedge. From my experience, a well maintained hedge requires consistent and regular trimming in order to gain the desired shape and stimulate the new growth required to keep it performing at its best. A thriving hedge is a true testament to the loving care of the gardener. In comparison a shrub left to its own devices becomes unstructured, scraggly and full of dead wood.

In *John 15:1-2* Jesus is talking about a spiritual vine, He tells us that He is like the vine, we (Christians) are like the branches and the Father in Heaven is the Divine Gardener. He talks about those branches which do not produce fruit being cut off and those which do produce being pruned or cut back in order to produce a greater abundance of fruit.

To tell you the truth, I have actually struggled with this verse and tonight I sat here asking God where does the line *"those which do not produce fruit being cut off"* stand in the light of grace and I struggle to reconcile the two. But nevertheless that is how it is written and because of its obscurity I believe that we need to take care that we do not flaunt the grace of God at the expense of fearing His holy and just nature.

I truly believe that we are saved by grace, that it is a free gift and that our right standing comes not through anything that we can do ourselves but through the righteousness of Christ who paid the price for our sins. Can we lose our salvation? I don't think anyone really knows for certain and I personally wouldn't dare to make a judgement on something I believe is reserved for Jesus alone.

But, here are some verses for you to consider:
- *Romans 11:17-24*
- *Galatians 5:4*
- *Hebrews 6:4-8*
- *Revelation 3:16*

- *Matthew 7:21-23*
- *John 10:28*
- *Romans 8:38-39*

Perhaps the implication of some of these verses lies in the *'realness'* of the conversion experience and the honesty and conviction of a truly repentant and fertile heart. Only the individual can know the true depth of their relationship with God and it is up to each person to work out their own salvation with *'fear and trembling'*. Yes God is the God of grace, but he is also Holy and Just. To me, *the natural outworking of a true conversion is the production of good fruit.* We cannot be truly attached to the Vine of Jesus without it impacting us in this way. The one thing I do know is that I never again want to find myself in a place where my salvation is questionable *I want to be a branch in the Vine that the Lord sees fit to prune.*

I will set my heart and soul to seek the Lord with all I have and with all I am that I might abide in Him and Him in me. That in Him and through Him I might live.

Pruning: Practical and Spiritual Applications *"... every branch that bears fruit, He prunes that it may bear more fruit."* There are many practical advantages to pruning in gardening:

- Pruning removes the dead wood: Spiritual pruning cuts those things from your life that are weighing you down and makes room for productive new growth.
- Pruning removes diseases and parasites: Likewise, God's pruning removes unhealthy thoughts and attitudes and habits that attach themselves to us without us realising.
- Pruning stimulates new growth: A stronger form and shape and a strong structure that is able to withstand strong winds. Likewise, spiritual pruning builds in us Christ-like character and a necessity to cling strongly to The Vine (Jesus) in order to sustain the storms and tempests of life.
- Pruning directs nutrients, moisture and energy to where it is needed most: To the production of abundant and sweet fruit rather than sustaining superfluous deadwood and showy greenery. Likewise, it removes the worldly distractions from our lives that cause us to waste time and energy on things that have no eternal value.
- Pruning invigorates and energises: Likewise, it creates renewed passion and zeal for the things of God in our lives as we see His glory and purpose revealed through our circumstances.

God prunes us because He loves us. He prunes us to help us grow to be more Christ-like, to strengthen and prove the mettle of our faith, to be more fruitful in our lives and in our relationships with both Him and with those around us. He has called us out of the world and into a new community that is underpinned by the strength of The Vine (Jesus). Our ability to produce fruit is dependent on our willingness to abide in the Vine and our confidence in the work of the Vinedresser (God the Father). For our life is in Him, our vitality is in Him, everything we are comes from Him—the Giver and Sustainer of life.

Job 33:4 *"The Spirit of God hath made me, and the breath of the Almighty hath given me life."*

When we remain in the Vine we remain under the covering of His love, compassion, care and grace. Sometimes love comes in the form of pain and sometimes growth can only be realised through pruning. The blade of God's Word is sharp and He knows the perfect time in which to prune the deadwood from our lives. When we allow Him to undertake His perfect work He makes it possible for us to endure the pain of His pruning that our branch might produce abundant and sweet fruit.

I once heard a sermon by a local preacher who preached on the **'Intent of the scalpel'**. This sermon has impacted me greatly. I cannot remember his exact words but they went something like this... *"If someone came at you with a scalpel, your first and natural reaction would be to run* *to avoid the pain it would inflict. But if you knew that the intention of the hand behind that scalpel was to perform an operation that would save your life, you would willingly submit and endure the pain knowing that the short term pain would achieve a much greater purpose."*

If God is allowing you to go through a season of great difficulty then it is quite possible that He has REALLY BIG plans for you. The true mettle of a person's faith can only be seen in the hard times and it is at these times too that the world will evaluate the value of our faith by our responses to suffering.

And finally

Have you ever seen a grapevine with just one branch? No! A grape vine is made up of many branches, all deriving their source from the Vine. So it is with believers. We are called to both be part of the Vine and also a productive member of the community of believers.

"Search me, O God, and know my heart; try me, and know my anxieties; and see if there is any wicked way in me; and lead me in the way of the everlasting."
Psalm 139: 23-24

THE CHALLENGE TO BE CHRIST-LIKE

Scripture of the week

2 Peter 1:3-4 *"...His divine power has given to us all things that pertain to life and godliness, through the knowledge of Him who calls us by glory and virtue, by which have been given to us exceedingly great and precious promises, that through these you may be partakers of the divine nature, having escaped the corruption that is in the world through lust."*

Prayer of the week

Father, I praise You that You have made available to me everything I require to live a life of Godliness. I praise You for the power of Your Spirit that guides and leads me, who convicts and teaches me. Thank You for Your Word that is filled with precious promises which remind me who I am in You. For the Sword of the Spirit which enables me to stand firm against the attacks of the enemy, and for the authority You have given me through Jesus Your Son. **AMEN**

Thought of the week
The challenge to be Christ-like

Quote:
"This Book (The Bible) *will keep you from sin;
or sin will keep you from this Book."*
(*John Bunyan*)

John 15:13 *"Greater love has no man than this; that a man lay down his life for his friends."*

Luke 23:34 *"Father forgive them, for they know not what they do."*

Is it possible to attain such love?

When each day is a struggle against selfish ambition and pride how can it be possible for anyone to come close to this sort of love, this sort of Christ-likeness?

But this is what we are called to do, to press on, to overcome the day to day challenges that life throws in our direction and embrace a new way of living, thinking, acting and responding. Each day bringing us into a deeper revelation of who Jesus is, so that others might see *"Christ in us."*

Whilst I still get frustrated by my perpetual weakness, I am learning that my life is a work in progress and it is through the brush strokes of life and through the struggles I face and overcome each day that the fullness of the knowledge of Christ is revealed in me—*one brush stroke, one struggle, one success at a time.*

Steps to growing in the knowledge of Christ - cultivating Christ-like graces

2 Peter 1:5-7 *"But also for this very reason"* (ie. from *v4*), *"giving all diligence"* (action, attention, devotion, constancy, exertions, energy).

STEP 1

"...add to your faith" (confident believing and assurance) - faith is the foundation, it is the first step towards the fullness of the knowledge of Christ Jesus our Lord.

STEP 2

"...virtue" (moral excellence)—**Wiktionary** describes virtue as *"the inherent power of a god, or other supernatural being"* - in other words it implies a willingness to allow the power of God to work in and through us.

STEP 3

"...to virtue knowledge" (awareness)—studying and understanding the Word of God so that you become informed and aware of how God desires for you to live. You have already been given the power at *Step 2*, now you need to learn who you really are, to tap into the source and to wield the sword that will ensure you stand firm and do not lose ground to the lusts of this world, *(verse 4).*

STEP 4

"...to knowledge self control" (temperance)—as the Word of God enlightens our hearts and minds, it takes discipline to actively apply those principles in our lives, to consistently resist the Devil that he would flee from us. To diligently stand in the knowledge of God's Word regardless of the battle going on around us. To remain righteous, allowing no place for the enemy to gain a foothold, *temperance enables us to resist sin.*

STEP 5

"...to self control perseverance" (patience)—the ability to persevere and steadfastly walk in the paths of righteousness according to the knowledge of God's Word that you would endure in times of trial, when the road seems long and unending and your physical body fails from the relentless attacks. It is the resolution to press on regardless.

STEP 6

"...to perseverance godliness" (pious conduct)—derived from devotion and a desire to please God because of the knowledge of Him that we have attained through His faithfulness to us, and His Word alive in us.

STEP 7

"...to godliness brotherly kindness" (charity or love for one another)–the 'overflowing' that happens when you are completely and totally immersed in the grace of God.

STEP 8

"... and to brotherly kindness love" (God is love and to love purely is to be Christ-like)—it is the pinnacle, the final and perfect expression of the fullness of the knowledge of Christ. For greater love has no man than this, that he would lay down his life for his friends... that is the ultimate expression of love, of 'Christ-likeness'.

God has given us everything we need to live a life of Godliness and He will never allow us to be tempted beyond that which we can bear. Our part is to put every effort (all diligence) into developing the Christ-like graces found in *2 Peter 1* until He returns again.

"If these things are yours and abound, you will be neither barren nor unfruitful in the knowledge of our Lord Jesus Christ."
2 Peter 1:8

WEEK 25

THE GARMENT OF PRAISE

Scripture of the week

Psalm 107:14 *"He brought them out of darkness the shadow of death, and broke their chains in pieces."*

Prayer of the week

Jesus, I come to You as my Deliverer. I confess that You are Lord and reject all influences of the enemy in my life. I confess my sins to You and choose now to lay them at Your cross, to turn away and leave them. I renounce any curses, occult or idolatry in my life or in the life of my ancestors. I forgive anyone who has ever hurt me in any way and I let go of any bitterness or resentment. I am saved by Your blood and Satan no longer has any legal authority over my life. You are the one true God and demons tremble at Your Name. I stand tall in the knowledge of who I am in You. I stand in agreeance with Your Word. Through Your blood I am justified. Through Your blood I am sanctified. Through Your blood, I am redeemed. **AMEN**

Thought of the week
My chains are gone

I want to share a couple of extracts from my journal. They are written approximately 18 months apart and reflect God's faithfulness even at a time when I stared directly into the face of death.

My desire is to inspire hope to those who have known despair... to paint a picture of the victory that comes from truly surrendering your heart to the higher calling of God. Much of my life has been sad, yes but God has taken those hurts, betrayals, abuses and despairs and replaced the ashes of my life with something beautiful in Him. Words cannot express my gratitude.

Isaiah 61:3 "To console those who mourn in Zion, to give them beauty for ashes, the oil of joy for mourning, the garment of praise for the spirit of heaviness; that they may be called trees of righteousness, the planting of the Lord that HE may be glorified."

EXTRACTS FROM MY JOURNAL

Extract 1: From hopelessness

"I sense another bout of sleepless nights. The restlessness is here again, that deep yearning for that which I can't define. I sit and watch with resignation as this life unfolds around me. Today there is no drive within me, just a deep unending mourning for a loss I can't describe. I want so much to close my eyes

and dream of places other than here but sleep evades me once again and the days drag on relentlessly.

Nothing moves me, I feel neither happy nor sad, just another nobody going through the motions and for what? I am not sure. I envy those who have gone. No pain, no remorse, no existence... just nothingness. Oh to experience that void and bliss.

I don't believe in love, I don't believe in people. I don't trust them or their motivations and agendas. At the end of the day they are motivated only by their human desire and need to avoid pain. I understand it but have no respect for it and yet, here we are all tarred with the same brush and for this I harbour self-loathing... weak, selfish and self-absorbed. How to break the cycle?

I can feel the anguish in my soul... a deep, heavy and restricted ball in my chest. Restricting my ability to breath and firmly lodged by my inability to cry... my nose runs and tears well up in my eyes but they never spill. Held back by unending self-control, afraid that to let one fall will open a gate that cannot be closed.

Afraid to go, afraid to stay, afraid of the sameness of my days. I think about dying every day, its presence fills the hours my mind is not consumed by work or sleep. I crave it, I fear it, I dream about it.

I am tired but no longer physically. This tired is older and more taxing. It is the tired of life's weariness, the tired that can only be quenched in death. I remain torn between the pull of life and death... the latter bearing greater witness as each new day emerges."

I was sitting in my bedroom and I couldn't sleep. I tossed and I turned and I struggled to fight an overwhelming sense of hopelessness and despair.

In desperation I picked up my Bible and it fell open at **Proverbs 24:11** and whilst the interpretation was not exactly correct in the context of the Scripture, it spoke to me regardless. ***"Deliver those who are drawn towards death,*** *and hold back those stumbling to the slaughter."*

I got up, determined to occupy my thoughts by sitting at my computer and working, but as I walked into the dark corridor of my house, I felt the Holy Spirit say to me *"You need to bind the spirit of heaviness."*

And that was all it took. As my mind acknowledged and agreed with the word planted in my heart, I physically felt a terrible burden lift from my shoulders. In the dark corridor of my home I had an encounter with God and my life since this time has changed beyond measure. My walk with God has become more intimate and I have an inner joy and peace that can only be described as a miracle in the context of my life.

I was going to write on spiritual oppression but instead I feel lead to just leave you with this second journal entry... I pray you will be uplifted and inspired to keep pressing on, to grasp that thread of hope when your world seems shrouded in darkness.

Extract 2: The garment of praise for the spirit of heaviness

"Lord, I praise You for the journey and for the joy I now find in You. You have brought me to a place of perspective—Your perspective. The things I once held valuable are no longer important and the longings of my heart have also changed and matured in You. I can finally look in the mirror and see a person of worth, a child of God in whose eyes I am precious.

I have 'touched the centre of my own sorrow [2]' and Lord, by Your grace have made it through, a better person because of it and in spite of it. 'Life's betrayals threatened to leave me closed and shrivelled [3]' but Your compassion and gentle beckoning has caused me to seek out and find hope and joy in the present and for the future. Thank You Lord for Your faithfulness."

The following is what God spoke to my heart:

"Fee, I heard your prayers, the cries and groaning's from the darkest places of your life. The times you felt so alone, when depression and dark thoughts threatened to consume you, when you were drowning

in confusion, abuse and hopelessness... I was there. I was that still, small voice, beckoning you away from the doors of death. The thread of hope that kept you pressing forward when all seemed in vain. I was your God then, as I am now. I will never leave you or forsake you, because you are precious to Me."

Psalm 34:4 *"I sought the LORD, and he answered me; he delivered me from all my fears."*

Psalm 9:9 *"The Lord also will be a refuge for the oppressed, A refuge in times of trouble."*

Psalm 116:8 *"For you have delivered my soul from death, my eyes from tears, and my feet from falling."*

WEEK 26

STIR UP THE GIFTS WITHIN YOU

Scripture of the week

2 Timothy 1:6-7 *"Therefore I remind you to stir up the gift of God which is in you through the laying on of my hands. For God has not given us a Spirit of fear, but of power and of love and of a sound mind.*

Prayer of the week

Thank You Father that You sent Your Holy Spirit to comfort and to guide us, to empower and enable us to live a life that is steeped in divine wisdom, divine insight and divine love and discernment beyond human reasoning. Inspire our words that they would impart life to those around us. Teach us to hear the voice of Your Spirit with clarity and assurance. In Jesus Name. **AMEN**

Thought of the week
Stir up the gifts within you

I was 22, two months pregnant and suddenly on my own. The words of *'worldy wisdom'* rang loudly in my ears. *"You're too young, it's too hard on your own, it will ruin your life... it's not too late to 'fix' it!"*... but the words of my heart rang louder and they fiercely sprang to the defence of the child growing in my womb and so, despite a growing and overwhelming fear of raising this child alone I rejected the 'well-intentioned' advice of 'well-intentioned' people.

It was not long after this time that I ventured into a church for the first time in a long time and it happened on that day that the words I heard as I sat down were from the story of David and Bathsheba, relaying how their infant died as a result of their sin of adultery. These were the only words I heard over and over again for the rest of the sermon and as I sat there, I was consumed with guilt, dread and condemnation. Because I didn't hear the whole sermon, I had formed a distorted understanding of the message presented and because I did not have a firm basis in scripture, I allowed the enemy to plant deception in my mind. I continued to attend church but for most of my pregnancy I was burdened by guilt and lived with a resigned belief that my child would be stillborn, deceptively persuaded that it was the price I would pay for my sin against God.

At around 8 months pregnant, I was sitting in church listening to a visiting speaker and at the end of the service he looked directly at me and asked me to come forward. The words he spoke shattered the yoke of the lie I had mistakenly believed and carried for so long. *"The Lord wants me to tell you that your child will live."* How could he have known if not for the Holy Spirit? I had not told a single soul but faced each day in silent grief for the judgement I believed I had brought upon my child. I praise God for this man's obedience to the voice of the Holy Spirit and for his faithfulness in delivering what would seem to many a very strange and dangerous message.

Words of knowledge—a gift of the Holy Spirit

This man was a complete stranger to me yet he knew the exact words to say that would set me free. It was not by his own knowledge that he spoke life into my situation but through the knowledge imparted to him by the Holy Spirit that dwells in him–the same Spirit that dwells in me, the same Spirit that dwells in you. You know Him and You know His voice. Listen with the ears of spiritual knowing and you will hear him speak directly to your heart. He will give you the tongue of the learned (knowing), *a word in season.*

John 10:27 *"My sheep hear My voice, and I know them, and I follow me."*

John 14:16-17 *"...I will pray the Father, and He will give you another Helper, that He may abide with you forever–the Spirit of truth, whom the world cannot receive, because it neither sees Him nor knows Him; but you know Him, for He dwells with you and will be in you."*

Matthew 10:19-20 *"But when they deliver you up, do not worry about what you should speak. For it will be given to* *you in that hour what you should speak; for it is not you who speak but the Spirit of the Father who speaks in you."*

Isaiah 50:4 *"The Lord God has given me the tongue of the learned, that I should know how to speak a word in season to him who is weary. He awakens me morning by morning, He awakens my ear to hear as the learned."*

I was young and inexperienced in my faith but the Lord used a complete stranger, someone with greater spiritual discernment and Biblical understanding to impart life giving words into my situation. Words that enabled me to move forward, one step closer to spiritual maturity and one step closer to the heart of the Father.

When we listen to the voice of the Spirit and the words He impresses on our hearts and then act on His prompting, He uses us to impart words that change lives. The same Holy Spirit that was in that itinerant minister is in you and I. He wants to use us to impart words of life to those around us. *"... for to one is given the word of wisdom, through the Spirit, to another the word of knowledge through the same Spirit..."* **1 Corinthians 12:8.** Why? To bring Glory to the Father; impart life to the Saints and; build faith in those who hear.

The Lord's Child... The child is now a man... dedicated to the Lord at birth. His first name means *'Of the right hand, Head of the House'* and his second means *'Judged by God'*. This is the poem I wrote to celebrate his birth ...

The Precious Gift

A tiny seed, a precious gift,
A treasure from above,
A secret parcel bound in life and
Sealed with God's own love.

Gentle flickers from within,
A child unique and dear.
A miracle of love and joy,
An answer to my prayers.

I praise you Lord with all I am
For this gift so undeserved.
I thank You for Your mercy Lord,
I thank You for Your love.

Lord protect my little child,
Encase him in Your love.
Teach him by Your Spirit Lord,
Equip his heart with joy.

May his laughter fill the lives,
of those filled with despair.
May he always know Your voice,
May he always care.

Bestow upon this tiny life,
A vision for the future.
Encompass him within Your truth,
Your wisdom, Your compassion.

Lord I pray You raise him up,
A mighty child of God.
May You be his Father, Lord
And guide him with Your love.

Felicity Eagan

WEEK 27

THE VOICE OF GOD

Scripture of the week

Romans 8:14 *"For as many as are led by the Spirit of God, these are sons of God."*

Prayer of the week

When I wake up. When I go to sleep. When I take each breath, Lord may I hear Your voice. When I come in and when I depart. When I am in the midst, may I hear Your voice. Lord I give it all, take what You will. But I pray, don't take Your voice. **AMEN**

Thought of the week
The voice of God

I have spoken often of *'hearing from God'* or *'the Holy Spirit impressed on me'* or *'I felt lead'* and I guess there are some who may be wondering... *"How do I really know if the voice I am hearing is God?"* Or *"Why can't I hear God's voice?"*

The Bible says *"My sheep hear My voice, and I know them, and they follow me."* **John 10:27**

I've had many a 'Jiminy Cricket' experience!

I guess I am blessed that by God's grace, I have always known His voice speaking directly to my heart. Right from a small child in Sunday school I felt a communion with Someone greater than myself, an inner knowing when something was the right thing to do and an inner turmoil when I wilfully acted against what I then thought was my 'instinct' or 'conscience'.

Perhaps the awareness of this inner voice stemmed from my being a quiet, introverted and reflective child. I largely preferred my own company to that of other people, and so spent many hours playing on my own. Stillness is the perfect forum in which to hear God speak.

It wasn't until many years later that I realised that this inner voice was actually that of the Holy Spirit guiding me, urging me... singing me home. In some of my darkest moments, the song I learnt in Sunday school... *'Yes, Jesus loves me'* came spontaneously into my mind and its words and familiar melody were a symbol of safety and security to me. The Holy Spirit was singing directly to my heart and bringing me comfort even then, even before I recognised the voice as His. And, it has only been in recent years that I have actively cultivated listening to God's voice and acted on the prompting of His Spirit.

Even more recently, I have commenced writing a two-way journal (as opposed to just me telling God all about my needs and wants) in which I deliberately bring myself to a point of stillness before Him and then when my eyes are fixed on Him, take my pen and spontaneously write everything down that flows into my mind... I do it without thinking, without analysing, untainted by my own thought processes. In fact, it often comes so fast I have trouble keeping up when writing it.

With fingers flying across the paper, God imparts such creative inspiration and words of wisdom through my journaling that I continually stand in awe of His great mercy... it is a powerful and I believe scriptural principal. The Psalmists wrote down their thoughts and God's responses to them and the Lord instructed Habakkuk to write on tablets the revelation that He gave to him.

Habakkuk 2:2-3 *"Write down the vision and make it plain on tablets so that he may run who reads it. For the vision is yet for an appointed time; but at the end it will speak, and it will not lie..."*

The reason that I am sharing this is that I believe it is so important for believers to know that YOU, as a child a God can and will hear His voice... if only you learn to close your ears and listen with your heart.

Tonight the voice of the Holy Spirit spontaneously filled my mind with what I am writing now and I just had to get it down on paper. The original topic for this message dropped into my heart a little while back but the content came only tonight as I felt impressed to pick up a book which I have wanted to read and which has been on my *"nice things to do"* list for months. As I flicked through the Appendix... the very message God had placed on my heart jumped out of the page (His perfect timing) and instigated this flood of words you are now reading.

The book I am talking about is *"Prayers that Heal the Heart"* by **Mark and Patti Verkler** and in it they speak about 4 keys to hearing Gods voice. I am going to share my thoughts on the first two.

Firstly, they mention that ***"God's voice in our hearts sounds like a flow of spontaneous thoughts"*** ... I believe God speaks to us through thoughts, visions, feelings or impressions. I cannot tell you how many times the name of a person has, from 'out of nowhere' dropped into my heart and I have felt lead to pray for them or call them or send them encouragement which the Lord has used to confirm, lift up or inspire them. It is only when we start to step out in faith and act on what we believe the Holy Spirit has placed on our heart, we become more conversant and confident in knowing and discerning His voice from amongst the myriad of other voices in our heads... i.e. self and the enemy.

What's the difference you say?

Well, from my experience the Holy Spirit doesn't scream. Now I am not saying that God doesn't raise His voice as there are incidences where He has audibly done so in the Old and New Testaments but when it comes to conversations of the heart, I have found that the Holy Spirit is generally the voice that is quietest, that demands the least and generally opts for gentle persuasion which (when you are really honest with yourself) 'resonates' perfectly within the depths of your heart—you will have peace about it. God is not a God of confusion, what He asks you to do will always line up perfectly with His word and will always bring edification... even when the words are words of caution... If it doesn't, you can be sure it is not of God.

Having said that, if the Holy Spirit really wants to get my attention about something He wants me to do and I'm not listening, I get a ball of urgency in my stomach that seems to grow more and more intense until I reach such a point that I need to be obedient or burst... but it still resonates perfectly, I still 'know' that it is the right thing to do but because, for whatever reason (generally fear or insecurity), I hesitate or put off his urging.

1 Corinthians 14:33 *"For God is not the author of confusion but of peace, as in all the churches of the saints."*

The second key mentioned is: **"I must learn to still my own thoughts and emotions, so that I can sense God's flow of thoughts and emotions within me"**... It's impossible to hear someone's voice clearly and without misinterpretation when your head is full of racket! We spend our days bombarded with information and juggling responsibilities. Somewhere in the midst of all of this we lose the propensity to hear God's voice even though it is innately built into our very being to do so. The secret is to learn to still your mind and if necessary, your body so that you are completely and utterly available to Him. (If the 'to do' list just won't leave you in peace then write down all those things you need to do and don't want to forget and then put it aside for later, so that you can focus all your attention on worshipping the Father without distraction).

For me singing to the Lord is a great way of settling my mind and focusing on Him. Sitting in the garden or walking in the bush or sitting on a cliff top overlooking the ocean are other great ways but admittedly not always accessible. Whatever you need to do to fix your eyes on Him do it, as it is so important, particularly when you are first starting out.

Expect Him to speak to you! Write down whatever comes into your mind... don't rationalise, just write. Write whatever you 'think' you hear, even if in the initial stages, a lot of what you write is 'self' initiated. You will feel clumsy and a bit self-conscious to start off with but remember, you are not writing a novel that the world is going to read, you are learning to intimately converse with your God and He will honour every effort you make to draw near to Him. You may want to burn the first volume (or you may just be surprised with the outcome) but regardless of the initial results, with practice you will get better until eventually His voice will be the default channel that your heart tunes into without a second or conscious thought. Eventually you will know His voice and you will hear His voice clearly–despite the chaos happening all around you.

Test and measure

Some ways to go back and measure if what you have heard or written is in line with the heart of God:

1. **Scripture***: 2 Timothy 3:16-17 "All Scripture is given by inspiration of God, and is profitable for doctrine, for reproof, for correction, for instruction in righteousness, that the man of God may be complete, thoroughly equipped for every good work."*

2. **Words of knowledge and Prophecy:** *1 Thessalonians 5:19-21 "Do not quench the Spirit; do not despise prophecies. Test all things; hold fast what is good."*

3. **Godly counsel:** *Proverbs 11:14 "Where there is no counsel, the people fall: but in the multitude of counsellors there is safety."*

4. **Independent confirmation:** *Matthew 18:16 "... by the mouth of two or three witnesses every word may be established.*

5. **The peace of God in your heart:** *Colossians 3:15 "Let the peace of God rule in your hearts, to which also you were called in one body; and be thankful."*

6. **Perfect Timing:** Things that just line up in time and space for Gods glory. *Acts 18:1-3 "After these things he* (Paul) *departed from Athens and went to*

Corinth. And he found a certain Jew named Aquila, a native of Pontus, who had recently come from Italy with his wife Priscilla, (because Claudius had commanded all the Jews to leave Rome); and He came to them. So, because he was of the same trade, he stayed with them and worked; for by occupation they were tent-makers."

"Your ears shall hear a word behind you, saying, "This is the way, walk in it," Whenever you turn to the right hand or whenever you turn to the left."
Isaiah 30:21

WEEK 28

WHAT IS THE CRY OF YOUR HEART?

Scripture of the week

Psalm 84:2 *"My soul longs, yes, even faints for the courts of the LORD; my heart and my flesh cry out for the living God."*

Prayer of the week

Search my heart, O Lord. Give me the courage to allow the scales of indifference to fall from my heart that You may plant within the tenderness revealed, a burden for the nations, a hunger for the kingdom. Instil in me a purpose that is birthed from a heart of compassion and motivated by love. **AMEN**

Thought of the week
What is the cry of your heart?

One Sunday morning, the Lord sent a missionary to our church and the message he shared changed my life forever.

I had been praying for direction that very morning and God answered the cry of my heart more powerfully than I could ever have dreamed. As I sat and listened He placed in me a seed of burden for a people group I knew little about. I knew at that very moment that my life would never be the same again, could never be the same again. A chord deep within me resonated with the voice of His calling and rang with a purpose and a vision that looked far beyond what I had imagined.

Pray for His direction in your life

"Where there is no revelation, (vision) *the people cast off restraint"* (Get side tracked and pre-occupied by worldly distractions or fall into sin). ***Proverbs 29:18***

The day before, I had been struggling to find direction in my life. That morning however, the Lord had captured my attention and as I allowed the scales of indifference to fall from my heart, He replaced it with a burden and a love for a people *'not my own'*.

I spent many hours afterwards seeking God, talking to people and researching all things related to the people, the country and the culture, to try and gain a greater understanding of what this burden meant. The more I learned, the greater the burden became and so began the journey I am now on. I never thought I would be around to witness the day that I would say...*"The Lord has called me to overseas Missions"* and yet here I am, preparing to go.

Proverbs 16:3 *"Commit your works to the Lord, and your thoughts* (plans) *will be established."*

A new perspective

So much of what I once thought important I now see as vanity—or as Solomon might say... *dust to the wind,* shallow and self-absorbed with little or no eternal value. A futile attempt at trying to find happiness and fulfilment outside of God... *I now have virtually nothing of earthly value and yet have never held such joy in my heart.*

I am utterly amazed at the speed in which God is effecting changes in my life, changes that are causing me to *'grow up'* and be *'freed up'* from personal, financial, emotional and physical bondages so that I might serve Him without distraction.

One by one and all in His timing the chains are being removed. Doors have opened that I haven't had to push and doors have closed that I am content to leave shut, without feeling the need to challenge its closure, without glancing back, without regret.

God will make a way

Isaiah 43:16-19 *"Thus says the Lord, who makes a way in the sea, a path in the mighty waters, who brings forth chariot and horse, the army and the power (They shall lie down together, they shall not rise; They are extinguished, they are quenched like a wick): Do not remember the former things, nor consider the things of old."*

Blessed Assurance

Exodus 13:21-22 *"And the Lord went before them by day in a pillar of cloud to lead the way, and by night in a pillar of fire to give them light, so as to go by day or night. He did not take away the pillar of cloud by day or the pillar of fire by night from before the people."*

Praise God! He has a plan and purpose for each of our lives although mine was not revealed until I made the choice to surrender my will to His. Perhaps my walk in the Lord would be further along now if I had made that decision earlier but I have learnt that it is pointless to have regrets for decisions not made. I choose instead to walk in the knowledge that He is doing a 'new' thing in me and now is His appointed time.

Habakkuk 2:3 *"For the vision is for an appointed time; but at the end it will speak and it will not lie. Though it tarries, wait for it! Because it will surely come."*

If you find yourself in unfamiliar territory remember, God is there... leading the way, giving guidance and direction. He brings light to the darkness; a way in the wilderness; a path in the mighty waters and; He quenches armies as easily as snuffing a candle. Such is His greatness!

Because He goes before us we can move confidently and sure-footedly through both the 'days' and 'nights' of our journey with Him. Surrender to Him and He will direct your paths. *"I do not count myself to have apprehended* (made it on my own); *but one thing I do: forgetting those things which are behind and reaching forward to those things which are ahead."* **Philippians 3:13.**

For I know that it is only through Him that...

> *"I can do all things because He strengthens me!"*
> **Philippians 4:13**

WEEK 29

OPEN OUR EYES THAT WE MAY SEE

Scripture of the week

2 Kings 6:17a "And Elisha prayed and said, "Lord, I pray, open his eyes that he may see." Then the Lord opened the eyes of the young man and he saw."

Prayer of the week

Lord, open my eyes that I might see. I do not need to live in fear or uncertainty for the battle is already won in You! And though armies might surround me; though circumstances threaten to swamp me; though the obstacles seem insurmountable, I will walk in the victory You made possible. I acknowledge Your sovereignty, I am empowered by Your great faithfulness, I am confident that in You and through You, all things are possible. I will praise Your Name always. **AMEN**

Thought of the week

Open our eyes that we may see

In **2 Kings 6** the servant of the Elisha trembled in fear as the army of the King of Syria assembled in great numbers on the horizon. Elisha saw his fear and said *"Do not fear,* *for those who are with us are more than those who are with them."*

Well! You can imagine what that servant must have been thinking, *"Elisha, are you for real? Perhaps you need a new set of glasses because from where I'm standing the future is not looking very bright!"*

Elisha, sensing his confusion prayed, ***"Lord open his eyes that he may see"***.

And at that moment he began to see, no longer with natural sight limited by distance and experience but with spiritual sight, limitless and without boundaries, eyes that could see beyond the circumstances; eyes that focused beyond his dire situation; eyes that beheld another aspect, another truth that he had never seen before and; eyes that brought confidence.

The servant did not see the Army of the Lord because he was not expecting to see it. He was spiritually blind and in his blindness only saw a dark vacancy that brought him to despair. But when looking through spiritual eyes he became aware of the Divine Presence of God and his perspective changed.

We often miss the opportunities God lays before us and walk straight past the doors He opens because we don't see them and we don't see them because we are not expecting them to be there. Whatever we ask for, we must walk expecting God to answer and to open doors and then, we must be prepared to walk through them in faith, being confident that He is in control of every situation regardless of the natural 'symptoms' that keep presenting.

In **John chapter 20**, Mary Magdalene mistook the risen Jesus as the gardener! Why? Because to her rational mind, Jesus was dead so it was not possible for Him to be standing before her. She was not expecting to see Him and so did not recognise Him. "Jesus said to her, *"Woman, why are you weeping? Whom are you seeking?" She, supposing Him to be the gardener, said to Him..."* **John 20:15a.**

In **Acts chapter 12**, the Angel led Peter out of the prison and took him to Mary's house where the disciples were in the process of praying for his release. They wouldn't open the door! Why? Because to their rational mind Peter was in prison, not standing at their door. *"It must be his Angel, they declared!"* God gave them an opportunity to open a door and they didn't recognise it. They didn't really expect God to answer their prayers or at least not in that timeframe.

(The girl) *"...ran in and announced that Peter stood before the gate. But they said to her, "You are beside yourself!" Yet she kept insisting that it was so. So they said, "It is his angel".* Now Peter continued knocking; and when they opened the door they were astonished. See *Acts 12:14b–16.*

If we are to walk in the type of faith that moves mountains then we need to start seeing the situations in our lives through God's eyes, spiritual eyes which recognise that nothing is impossible with God and if nothing is impossible for God then all things are possible for you.

Mission impossible?

An impotent man, a withered womb... *mission impossible*? Abraham was an old man when he fathered Isaac, his body was considered 'dead' and Sarah was effectively barren. Yet, Abraham believed in that which seemed impossible (the symptoms actually dictated that it was not physically possible). He chose to ignore the natural and believed in the supernatural and by faith he held on to the promise that he would be the father of many nations and God brought to pass the 'impossible'.

Romans 4:17b-21 *"God, who gives life to the dead and calls those things which do not exist as though they did who, contrary to hope, in hope believed* (even though in the natural it seemed hopeless, he (Abraham) chose to trust the Word of His God) *so that he became the father of many nations, according to what was spoken, "So shall your descendants be.* (God fulfilled the 'impossible' promise) *And not being weak in faith, he did not consider his own body, already dead (since he was about 100 years old) and the deadness of Sarah's womb.* (Faith destroying symptoms). *He did not waver* (choice) *at the promise of God through unbelief, but was strengthened in faith, giving glory to God, and being fully convinced that what He had promised He was also able to perform."* Abraham knew his God had integrity, that his God did not lie *(Numbers 23:19)* and that he could have complete confidence in the word of His Lord even when natural circumstances dictated otherwise.

Proverb 3:5-6
"Trust in the Lord with all your heart
Lean not on your own understanding
In all your ways acknowledge Him
And He shall direct your paths."

Matthew 17:20 *"...I say to you, if you have faith as a mustard seed, you will say to this mountain* (this army, this seemingly insurmountable obstacle) *"Move from here to there, and it will move."* Expect it, walk in it, even though you can't see it, knowing that the battle has already been won *and nothing will be impossible for you.*

WEEK 30

THE GREATEST LOVE STORY

Scripture of the week

John 14:2 *"In my Father's house there are many mansions; if it were not so I would have told you. I go to prepare a place for you."*

Prayer of the week

Jesus, I thank You that because of You, I play a lead role in the greatest love story this world has ever known and that through You, I am justified and made righteous. The filthy rags of my sinful nature have been cast off and replaced with the pure white linen of righteousness. My heart yearns for Your return for the day when I will sit beside You at the table of our wedding feast and know that in You I am set free to walk in wholeness, purity and liberty. May You be praised! My King of Kings, my Lord of Lords, my Husband, my Redeemer. **AMEN**

Thought of the week
A little girl's dream

It is every little girls dream to find her prince charming, her knight in shining armour. To be swept away on the wings of love and live happily ever after! Dreams do come true, we just need to correctly fill in the gaps. Now those who are cynical amongst us might say, phooey! Because, somewhere in the midst of dirty nappies, sound breaking snoring and smelly socks (not to mention a whole heap of other 'unmentionables'), the dream you once held became eroded in the day to day struggle of just getting through and somewhere along the way you have shut down and closed your mind to what might be. The hope you once held is now lost to just a childhood fantasy and you silently whisper to yourself... *"this isn't what I signed up for!"*

Tragic miscommunication

Somewhere along the way we got our wires crossed. The fairy tale books of *'happily ever after'* actually do hold an element of truth, but fail to enlighten little girls on the *'dirty sock'* bits that fill in the gaps between *'prince charming'* and *'the end'*.

And so our expectations are distorted and only partially based in truth. It is not all flowers and rose petals, but hard work and commitment. ***God intended for marriage to be an instrument of perfecting, not an instrument of perfection.*** His intention was for a man and woman to come together in a Godly covenant between two individuals whose first love is Him. Individuals who complement each other and who actively love and respect each other. Two people moving with a Christ centred focus, a calling greater than the sum of either of them and with a purpose attainable only through Christ who lives in them.

God designed marriage between a man and a woman in order:

- To build each other up and to encourage each other to be the best that they can be in life and in faith.
- To love each other's bodies as they love their own.
- To support each other in the hard times and to remind each other of the vision when the drudgery of life threatens to swamp it.
- To carry one another through sorrow and times of separation and to share the burden of life when it is just too great for the shoulders of one.
- To extend the grace of Jesus and to accept each other's failings without judgement.
- To see beyond the visible flaws to the potential hidden within and to love each other in spite of our failings.
- To pray each other through the deep inner struggles and to fight beside them during spiritual battles, to usher them through prayer into the victory found in Christ. A union of Godly leadership and submission in which both husband and wife are equal heirs to Gods kingdom.

"...they are no longer two but one flesh." **(Matt 19:5)**

It is when we allow God to be Lord of our union He teaches us about unconditional love, about respect, honour, tolerance and perseverance. He provides the grace to forgive and be forgiven and through this covenant of love, we learn to serve and esteem others greater than we esteem ourselves.

The Church is the Bride of Christ and He is our Groom

HE IS COMING BACK... To take us to the place that He has prepared for us. He died that we would be made righteous that He could present us to His Father faultless and without spot, so that we might live in His house forever. This is the greatest love story on earth. This is the story we need to teach our children. *For their hope of glory is in Christ alone.* **(see Colossians 1:27)**

THE GREATEST LOVE STORY EVER

Take heart fair maiden... Your Prince is coming! He is coming back for YOU, His bride. For you who believe in Him, and in that day He will carry you over the threshold to the place He has prepared for you. And when He comes, you will be changed and made perfect *in the twinkling of an eye,* **(see 1 Corinthians 15:51-55)**. No more will you wander the streets lost and without hope, no longer will you wallow in the filth and slime of your sinful life, for your bridegroom comes to redeem you and you will dwell with Him in His Father's house forever. You will bask in His glory and in the fullness of His love forevermore. Stand strong and with courage fair maiden because for a short while you must experience this time of separation—it is a time for preparation and for spiritual adornment. Remember*"...a gentle and quiet spirit is very precious in the sight of God"* **(1 Peter 3:4)**

Your Groom knew that the road to purity would not be easy but He also knew that the trials you would face would build character and inner beauty attainable by no other means. So, out of love for you He asked His Father to send you a Chaperone, a Helper who would guide you and cause you to walk in the paths of righteousness that you might become holy just as He is holy. His name? The Holy Spirit! And it is His charge to enable you to continue the work of your betrothed in His absence and to provide you also with the fortitude and the strength of character to be upright and faithful in a deceitful and menacing world. May the inner cry of your heart beat in time with that of your Beloved. And may His presence surround you, though for a short time you see him not.

Fair maiden do you not know that in your waiting, your heart grows fonder? Declare his coming to those who don't know Him, even as you wait for your Bridegroom and yearn for His return. *(see 2 Timothy 4:8)*. And the maiden replied, *"As I wait, I will yearn for my Bridegroom but for now, in His absence I will be faithful. I will keep the home fires burning and I will declare his imminent return. I will place a lamp on a stand beyond the doors of my dwelling and I will pray that its light might draw weary travellers to its warmth, that they may know and taste of His love and compassion which abides within these walls."*

So for now fair Maiden, while you wait for this *'blessed hope'* *(see Titus 2:11-13)*, may you stand firm in the Grace of God and in the example of your beloved, who through His life brought honour to His Father and through His death and resurrection brought hope and restoration to the lost.

Arise Fair Maiden, Your Prince returns! Know that your filth has been washed away and you have been cleansed *'whiter than snow' (see Isaiah 1:18)*. Your rags have been stripped and replaced with royal and righteous garments of *'white linen' (see Revelation 19:8)* and the Groom has returned for His bride.

The glorious *'King of Kings and Lord of Lords' (see Revelation 19:16b)* comes *'mounted on a white horse' (see Revelation 19:11)*. He is called *'faithful and true'* and He is *'crowned with many crowns' (see Revelation 19:11-12)*. He is glorious to behold and He returns to claim you, His bride. He wraps you in the wings of His love and restores you to your place at his side. And on the day of your marriage feast, the voice of a great multitude will declare... *"Alleluia! For the Lord God Omnipotent reigns! Let us be glad and rejoice and give Him glory, for the marriage of the Lamb has come, and His wife has made herself ready." (Revelation 19:6a-7)*

And the Maiden and her Beloved truly did live happily ever after.

-The End-

"For your Maker is your husband, the Lord of Hosts is His name; and your Redeemer is the Holy One of Israel; He is called the God of the whole earth."
Isaiah 54:5

WEEK 31

OUT OF THE ASHES

Scripture of the week

Isaiah 48:10 *"Behold, I have refined you, but not as silver; I have tested you in the furnace of affliction."*

Prayer of the week

Lord, today I choose to smile. I choose to smile at the dishes in the sink because their existence reminds me that You have provided food for my table. I choose to smile at the laundry in the basket for it reminds me that You have clothed me. I chose to smile when I pass by the empty chair because it reminds that their life brought joy to my heart. I choose to smile when I am suffering because it reminds me that You suffered also. I choose to smile when I am faced with adversity because I know that it will cause me to seek Your face. I choose to smile, Lord secure in the knowledge that You are my strength and my joy. **AMEN**

Thought of the week
Reminders of loss

The recent fires in and around my home town devastated the landscape bordering the road on which I travel to and from work.

The charred remains of leafless trees, twisted road signs and blackened dirt was all that remained—such was the intensity of the heat and flames. Each day I pondered and mourned the loss, the scorched backdrop serving as a glaring reminder of the fragility of life.

A smile from within the ashes

This morning I looked beyond the black that dominated my view and I smiled. Life might be fragile but it is also resolute and tenacious and in stark contrast to the blackened darkness, pockets of green danced defiantly in the breeze—out of the ashes sprung life!

Lessons from creation

The seeds of the Banksia plant lay dormant for years and come to life only on the day the old plant dies. The old life is sacrificed for the new and from adversity springs life. The seed's regeneration is dependent on the intensity of fire (adversity) to release it from its seed pod and the combined elements of extreme heat and permeating smoke are crucial in providing it with the stimulus it needs to germinate and flourish.

Adversity causes the seams of its containment to break open and reveal the potential for new growth within. The smoke permeates its very being causing the seed to quicken and grow. The seed takes root and becomes established until finally after many years of weathering, it reaches maturity and the cycle continues.

So it is with us. There are qualities in our lives that can only be attained through the refinement and adversity of life's fires and lessons such as patience, perseverance and long-suffering can be attained by no other means.

1 Peter 4:12-13 "Beloved, do not think it strange concerning the fiery trail which is to try you, as though some strange thing has happened to you; but rejoice to the extent that you partake of Christ's sufferings, that when His glory is revealed, you may also be glad with exceeding joy."

How can we hunger for peace if we have never known conflict? How can we recognise hope if we have never experienced despair? The true value of joy can only be understood when you have experienced sorrow. The true depth of love can only be understood when you have lived despised.

The bible says that the Lord gave Israel *"...the valley of Achor* (Trouble) *as a door of hope;" **Hosea 2:15b***

He knew that in the valley of trouble Israel would look to Him for salvation. That they would seek Him out and repent from their idolatress hearts. That they would draw near to Him and turn their eyes towards Him in hope. That He might have mercy and restore them to Himself.

I pray that you will look to Him for strength to move beyond the circumstances... beyond the sorrow, beyond the loneliness, beyond the piling bills and the daily struggle. That you would praise God for the work of refinement that He is perfecting in your life. And, may you *joy* in the lessons and wisdom that are borne of struggle.

"My brethren, count it all joy when you
fall into various trials, knowing that
the testing of your faith produces patience"
James 1:2-3

WEEK 32

LESSONS FROM A HEADLESS CHICKEN

Scripture of the week

Isaiah 53:5d "...and by His stripes we are healed."

Prayer of the week

Lord, I pray today for a revelation to my heart that unveils the stumbling blocks which prevent me from walking in the fullness of faith and Your healing power. Your Word says that faith comes by hearing and hearing by the word of God, so Lord I pray that as I meditate on Your word that You would embed Your truth in my heart, for Your Word is life! In Jesus name. **AMEN**

Thought of the week
Lessons from a headless chicken

For over 18 months I struggled with a shoulder injury that restricted my movement and caused me great pain and discomfort. My 'quest' for healing consumed me and no matter what I did, no matter what I confessed, no matter what I declared, something inside me kept sabotaging my attempts to believe. I *'wanted'* to believe but the ever present symptoms plagued me and I couldn't see through them.

God's Word is constant and relevant across generations

Hebrews 13:8 *"Jesus Christ is the same yesterday, today and forever".*

It was His desire to heal then and I believe it is His desire to heal today. ***Isaiah 53*** indicates that by His stripes we *'are'* healed or *'were'* healed. In no translation can I find *'will be'* healed and to me this indicates that the work has been done, it is finished! Simplistically, it could be said that all that is left to do is have faith that the work *has* been done, accept it and *walk in it in spite of the symptoms*. I could declare it as much as I liked but until I 'accepted' it as 'truth' I would never walk in its reality.

Walking in the Truth

A gory story...

When I was younger, a family friend used to kill and dress his own chickens. I was allowed to watch one day and stood by solemnly as the chickens were laid one by one over the chopping block. I froze in horror as their headless bodies raced frantically around the back yard before finally slowing and coming to a standstill.

The friend didn't appear to even notice their antics, he just let them do their thing and focused his attention back to the task at hand. He must have realised my concern and said without even looking up, *"Don't worry they can't feel anything, they're already dead, they just haven't realised it yet."*

The *'reality'* for those poor chickens was that they *were* actually dead (even though to me they looked very much alive and scary). But dead they were, it just took a few minutes for the nerves in their bodies to catch up and align themselves to that truth. I was grateful when they eventually lost momentum and finally came to a standstill.

Now relating this back to my shoulder! It was at the point that I stopped focusing on what *'appeared to be reality'* (the symptoms of my shoulder injury) and decided to *'carry on'* and push through in spite of it that I made progress. I had allowed the *'headless chicken'* of pain to distract me from my purpose and was running around trying to calm it rather than accepting and walking in the 'truth' of my situation (my healing in Christ). All I really needed to do was to change my focus from the obvious distraction of the *'headless chicken'* and calmly get on with the job God had asked of me knowing that the physical symptoms had no alternative but to come into line with the spiritual reality of my situation.

In choosing to keep my mind on the task rather than be distracted by the sideshow of my pain I was able to stay focused and productive. One day it dawned on me that the pain was gone and I hadn't even noticed. Today I am pain free and I praise God that I never had to endure the surgery I was told I would.

The gift

Someone once said to me that receiving healing is like someone giving you a gift. The gift is there, the price has been paid to purchase it and the giver holds it before us waiting for us to reach out and receive it. We actually need to accept the gift before it can have any impact in our lives. But, rather than taking the word of the giver that the gift is good, we stand there and rationalise it... *"Should I take the gift? Why would you buy a gift for me? Give it to someone who needs it more. It does look lovely! It looks expensive. I don't really deserve it! You really brought that for me? Seriously? I really would like that gift! But I don't know..."*

Unless we choose to accept that the gift is a reality and then step out in faith and receive the gift, we will never know what's inside that box or really experience the fullness of its contents in our lives.

Searching for the Truth

So if, *"Faith comes by hearing and hearing by the Word of God"* **Romans 10:17**, then it makes sense to immerse ourselves in the Word and in scriptures that bear witness to the truth of His healing power, prayerfully asking the Holy Spirit to quicken and establish that truth in our hearts so that we can walk in it regardless of the circumstances and symptoms that threaten to distract us.

WEEK 33

IN WHOSE HANDS DO YOU TRUST?

Scripture of the week

Psalm 63:8 *"My soul follows close behind You; Your right hand upholds me."*

Prayer of the week

Lord, take my hand. I purposely relinquish my right hand to You. May Your will be done in me. May Your will be done through me. Not by my own power or authority, but by Your power and authority. May Your Name be lifted up. May the nations praise You. May You be glorified in our lives. In Your precious name. **AMEN**

Thought of the week

In whose hands do you trust?

I am not normally a person who gets dreams and visions, for me they are rare but driving to work one day the Lord blessed me with a vision. Actually, it was two visions played simultaneously across the screen of my mind and as they did so an unspoken question lodged itself in my heart... *"When the time comes, which will you choose?"*

Reaching up

I groaned to myself and thought *"does this mean I am heading for a fall?"* But as I reflected further I realised that this was not a warning of impending doom but a treasured moment of clarity and resolve, a moment that the Holy Spirit will inevitably draw on and use to remind me in whom my hope lies during the times when my own strength fails me.

The vision

I was standing on a precipice with a storm blowing fiercely all around me I was blinded by the rain and was being pushed and tossed until finally I became unbalanced and I realised fearfully I was about to fall. The vision suddenly broke into two parallel visions and I knew in that instant that I only had but a second to choose one of two paths.

As I watched I saw the consequences of each vision play out before me. In the first I stretched out my arms and used my hands to break the fall. I watched in horror as I hit the ground and my wrists snapped and broke with the weight of the impact, leaving me helpless, vulnerable and in pain.

In the second vision I also began to fall but as I felt my feet slide out from underneath me I turned without thinking and reached upward and as I did so I grasped the right hand of God. By clinging to His right hand I was able to regain my footing and walk upright and with confidence as sure-footed as a deer on the cliff-tops he guided me safely through the tempest.

Symbolism of the 'right hand'

As I have searched the scriptures and read commentaries, I have become aware of the symbolism of the right hand... The *"right hand"* denotes:

- **Power** (Ps 89:13, Ps 45:4; Ps 77:10; Isa 62:8; Ps 118:15-16; Isa 48:13)
- **Protection** (Ps 16:8; Ps 63:8; Ps 139:10; Isa 41:13; Lam 2:3)
- **Victory** (Ps 18:35; Ps 78:54; Isa 41:10, Ex 15:6; Ex 15:12; Ps 21:8)
- **Judgement** (Lam 2:4; Hab 2:16)
- **Authority** (1Pet 3:22; Eph 1:20-21; Ps 80:15; Ps 98:1; Ps 138:7)

The right hand OF GOD

Psalm 139:10 *"Even there Your hand shall lead me, and Your right hand shall hold me."*

When we reach out and take the right hand of God we are plugging into the power, protection, victory, judgement and authority of our Creator. It doesn't matter where we are or what we do, the Spirit of the Lord is with us. If we ascend into Heaven *He is there*, if we make our bed in Hell *He is there*, if we dwell in the depths of the sea *He is there* and even in the dark times, *He is there*!

When we reach out and take His hand, He leads us to safety and to victory, He gives us strength when we have nothing left to draw on and, He stops us leaning on our own understanding which would inevitably lead to 'broken' bones and prolonged pain.

The right hand OF MAN

In my research, I also found scriptures referring to *'our'* right hand and it left me puzzled. I searched and I pondered and I drew a blank. If reference to the 'right hand' symbolises power and authority why would the scriptures talk about *'our'* right hands? When I looked closer at the verses that made reference to our right hand, I noticed that God was generally holding our hand. ***Light bulb moment!*** The way I see it, if God is holding or controlling your hand, it is pretty difficult to use it to achieve your own purposes.

Now I am not a theologian but perhaps when we allow God to take us by the 'right hand' we are also saying to Him *"I choose to relinquish my 'right hand' power and authority in order that Your 'right hand' power and authority can work in and through me."*

Isaiah 41:13 *"For I the Lord, your God, will hold your right hand, saying to you, 'Fear not, I will help you.'"*

Psalm 73:23 *"Nevertheless I am continually with You; You hold me by my right hand."*

Psalm 16:8 *"I have set the Lord always before me; because He is at my right hand, I shall not be moved."*

What happens when we place our right hand in the right hand of God?

When we submit to the right hand of the Lord, He is glorified in us. When the lost see the work that He is able to achieve in and through us regardless of life's storms, our lives become a light to the nations, the eyes of the blind are opened and the prisoners are set free.

> *"I, the Lord, have called You in righteousness,*
> *and will hold Your hand.*
> *I will keep You and give You as a*
> *covenant to the people, as light to*
> *the Gentiles, to open blind eyes, to bring*
> *out prisoners from the prison,*
> *those who sit in darkness from the prison house."*
> **Isaiah 42:6-7**

WEEK 34

PRAISE GOD! I'M OUT OF CONTROL!

Scripture of the week

Luke12:25 "And which of you by worrying can add one cubit to his stature?" (some versions say *'a single hour to his life'*).

Prayer of the week

In all things, Lord may I kneel humbly before Your throne in prayer. In all things, Lord may I seek the wisdom of Your perfect counsel. In all things, Lord may I seek Your will and heart's desire. In all things, Lord may Your kingdom come. In Jesus Name. **AMEN**

Thought of the week
Praise God! I'm out of control!

They say, (don't ask me who *'they'* are but I have heard that *'they'* say) that your chosen study or career path is often a direct reflection of your personality.

Well, given I have qualifications in Administration and Event Management I am guessing that there is a fairly high probability that I fall into the category of being a bona fide CONTROL FREAK! (It also indicates that I am organised and productive but for the purposes of this exercise I am going to focus on the 'control freak' aspect).

Anyone who knows me well will tell you that I have a place for everything and everything in its place. I like to tick all the boxes. I line all my ducks neatly in a row. I like to know where I'm going and how I am going to get there. I will no doubt have a carefully structured plan and a water-tight contingency. Not to mention a fairly advanced system of reminders that remind me to remind others when their contribution to my project is due. I know how to get things done and if I agree to undertake a task I will do whatever is necessary to get it done and meet deadlines. Finally, I like to be on time! In fact, on time for me is at least 10 minutes early.

The best laid plans

One particular day, I had a 12.30 lunch appointment. I had made the restaurant booking weeks earlier. I facilitated an appropriate time and place, sent out details and final reminders and allowed plenty of time to get there. Yep! *I had it all under control...*

Well, you can imagine my dismay when 12.30 came and went and we were still fifteen minutes away from the destination! I felt the anxiety start to well up inside me, I couldn't stop to text and we were going to be late! To compound matters, the restaurant was not in the place I thought it was, so we parked too far away and then had to re-adjust our geographical coordinates in order to find the right location.

Now you may be reading this and saying *"It's good to plan to be on time and to be concerned that people are waiting for you"* and from a stewardship perspective, I wholeheartedly agree. But as I sit writing this I wonder what value I gained in being anxious and raising my blood pressure, over nothing more than a 15 minute miscalculation. *I wonder about the value of 'sweating the small stuff'.*

So, there I was furiously marching up the street trying to regain a couple of lost minutes, and all I could think was **"Who of you by worrying can add a single hour to your life?".** *"Girl, you need to get a grip! Why are you getting all hot under the collar about being 15 minutes late? Sure, it's not ideal but seriously? It is NOT the end of the world!"*

So really, this message is not about me being late or early or even on time but more about what is and what isn't actually important and beneficial to the kingdom and in what activities I choose to invest my energy. If I had taken 2 minutes and looked at this situation rationally, I would have realised that there is absolutely no value in pouring energy into negative emotions triggered by something that cannot be changed and which, when all is said and done, has no eternal value.

Now don't get me wrong here. I am not condoning that we blatantly disregard other people's lives and schedules but it is impossible to foresee every potential problem and sometimes through circumstances we can't control things just don't go to plan. The reality is *you are not going to change the unchangeable by worrying!*

In the larger context, my little lunchtime meltdown is an anecdote of a far greater picture.

The Bible says, *"Be anxious for nothing, but in everything by prayer and supplication, with thanksgiving, let your requests be made known to God." **Philippians 4:6***

I am guessing there is a really good reason this verse and others like it is in the Bible... *anxiety is not of God.* In fact, in this verse He tells us to hand it over to Him by prayer and supplication and thanksgiving. If we are to be productive and effective in the work God has for us, we need to learn to not *'sweat the small stuff'*. Worry robs us of our energy, it robs us of our joy and it takes our focus away from what is truly important.

So as you ponder this little story, I pray that the Holy Spirit might also make you aware of the things in your life that cause you to be anxious and over which you have no control. May you know the joy that comes from casting all of your cares on Him having confidence that in everything (even the small stuff), He is in control. And as you hand the reins over to Him, may you walk in the freedom that comes from being able to say ***Praise God! I'm out of control!***

"...casting all your care upon Him for He cares for you."
1 Peter 5:7

WEEK 35

FORGIVENESS– GRACE IN ACTION

Scripture of the week

Psalm 86:5 *"For You, Lord, are good, and ready to forgive, and abundant in mercy to all those who call upon You?"*

Prayer of the week

Lord, teach my heart to move to the beat of a different drum. Give me a revelation of Your heart towards those who are lost and hurting. Bring me to a point where Your hearts cry is greater than the cry of my own heart that I would be moved with compassion and love for those who don't know You. **AMEN**

Thought of the week

Forgiveness—grace in action

I doubt that there are any among us that have not experienced pain and hurt in our lives and who have as a result, harboured grudges, built up walls and made silent vows soaked in revenge. Sometimes our hurts are as a result of offences inflicted directly on us, sometimes against those we love and sometimes against nothing more than our sense of justice. But we want them to hurt. We want them to be accountable. We want them to pay for the pain that they have caused. But... **you are called to walk to the beat of a different drum!**

And it is only when we start to see those who have hurt us through the eyes of Jesus that we can really begin to understand the rhythm, *the heartbeat of the Father.* Without Christ our forgiveness will never be fully complete. We may attain a level of success but somehow we are never fully free from the feelings that cause us to react negatively whenever we think about or come face to face with the offender. We don't like the pain it causes us, or the bile it brings to our throat. It has the power to make our heart weary, it steals our energy and it can cause us to be physically ill. So, in a desperate attempt to find release, we sanctimoniously bury it beneath the surface with the intent of putting it *'out of mind and out of site'* only to have it reach up and grab us by the ankle, incapacitating us when we least expect it.

Often un-forgiveness cripples you far more than the person towards whom you hold hatred in your heart. True, they may be hurting also, but chances are they are not even aware of the offence and are blissfully living their lives totally unaware of your pain. Meanwhile you smoulder and seethe until it consumes you and permeates every part of your being, until eventually you cannot see or think of anything else. I have been in this place and every part of me shrieked *"I will make you pay"*, *"I will show you what it feels like"*. All it did was consume me. It made me sick. It stole my joy and it robbed me of peace.

The journey to forgiveness is not an easy one and it takes courage and strength that can only be found outside the realms of our own capability. It is when we immerse ourselves in Him and shift our eyes from self to the 'reason' for the cross that we can truly understand the power of redemption and of His forgiveness. When we choose, in obedience to His Word, to forgive we extend the same grace to others that Christ outspread to us. When through His strength, we make a conscious decision to put aside our own rights in response to His higher call, we show **grace in action.** When we choose to bless instead of curse **we disempower the enemy.**

And then one day when you least expect it, the forgiveness that started as an act of will, becomes a position of the heart and the sting has lost its power. Suddenly, without you even realising, you will be able to think about that person and you will see them in a different light, a light that illuminates their deep need and their human frailty and you will have compassion—*compassion that can only come from Christ.*

What is forgiveness?

Forgiveness is a command
Ephesians 4:31-32 *"Let all bitterness, wrath, anger, clamour, and evil speaking be put away from you, with all malice. And be kind to one another, tender-hearted,*

forgiving one another, even as God in Christ forgave you."

Forgiveness invites forgiveness
Matthew 6:14-15 *"For if you forgive men their trespasses, your heavenly Father will also forgive you. But if you do not forgive men their trespasses, neither will your Father forgive your trespasses."*

Forgiveness cleanses
1 John 1:9-10 *"If we confess our sins, He is faithful and just to forgive us our sins and to cleanse us from all unrighteousness. If we say that we have not sinned, we make Him a liar, and His word is not in us."*

Forgiveness benefits the forgiver
Isaiah 43:25-26 *"I, even I, am He who blots out your transgressions for My own sake; and I will not remember your sins. Put Me in remembrance; let us contend together; state your case, that you may be acquitted."*

Forgiveness brings refreshing
Acts 3:19 *"Repent therefore and be converted, that your sins may be blotted out, so that times of refreshing may come from the presence of the Lord,"*

Forgiveness is an act of grace
Ephesians 1:7 *"In Him we have redemption through His blood, the forgiveness of sins, according to the riches of His grace."*

Forgiveness opens the channel of prayer
Mark 11:25 *"And whenever you stand praying, if you have anything against anyone, forgive him, that your Father in heaven may also forgive you your trespasses. But if you do not forgive, neither will your Father in heaven forgive your trespasses."*

Forgiveness is a sign of God's elect
Colossians 3:12-14 *"Therefore, as the elect of God, holy and beloved, put on tender mercies, kindness, humility, meekness, longsuffering; bearing with one another, and forgiving one another, if anyone has a complaint against another; even as Christ forgave you, so you also must do. But above all these things put on love, which is the bond of perfection."*

Forgiveness has no limits
Matthew 18:21-22 *"Then Peter came to Him and said, "Lord, how often shall my brother sin against me, and I forgive him? Up to seven times?" Jesus said to him, "I do not say to you, up to seven times, but up to seventy times seven.""*

Forgiveness disarms the Devil
2 Corinthians 2:10-11 *"Now whom you forgive anything, I also forgive. For if indeed I have forgiven anything, I have forgiven that one for your sakes in the presence of Christ, lest Satan should take advantage of us; for we are not ignorant of his devices."*

Forgiveness bewilders
Luke 6:27-28 *"But I say to you who hear: Love your enemies, do good to those who hate you, bless those who curse you, and pray for those who spitefully use you."*

Forgiveness is an act of reconciliation
Proverbs 17:9 *"He who covers a transgression seeks love, but he who repeats a matter separates friends."*

Forgiveness willingly forfeits the right to judge
Romans 12:18-19 *"If it is possible, as much as depends on you, live peaceably with all men. Beloved, do not avenge yourselves, but rather give place to wrath; for it is written, "Vengeance is Mine, I will repay," says the Lord."*

Forgiveness extends mercy
Acts 7:59-60 *"And they stoned Stephen as he was calling on God and saying, "Lord Jesus, receive my spirit." Then he knelt down and cried out with a loud voice, "Lord, do not charge them with this sin." And when he had said this, he fell asleep."*

Forgiveness is a choice with eternal consequences
Matthew 18:35 *"So My heavenly Father also will do to you if each of you, from his heart, does not forgive his brother his trespasses."*

WEEK 36

THE GRASS IS NOT GREENER, JUST WARMER!

Scripture of the week

Ephesians 1:17-18 "*...that the God of our Lord Jesus Christ, the Father of glory, may give to you the spirit of wisdom and revelation in the knowledge of Him, the eyes of your understanding being enlightened; that you may know what is the hope of His calling, what are the riches of the glory of His inheritance in the saints.*"

Prayer of the week

Lord help me to be gracious in the words that I speak and in the way I handle and respond to words that are spoken to me. Give me discernment to know when to accept and when to reject words spoken over me and to me. Give me wisdom to understand who I am in You and to walk in the truth of that Your word says about me. **AMEN**

Thought of the week

The grass is not greener, just warmer!

At 14 I left home and moved interstate. I realise now that I was running in an attempt to outrun my past and escape my present. In my young mind things would <u>have</u> to be better where the weather was warmer and the people more laid back. Well, let me tell you something! *People are the same no matter where you run and problems still find their way to warm climates.*

I didn't know myself any better in the new location than I did in the old. My fears and insecurities remained the same, my perception of who I was (or wasn't) didn't change with the scenery and all I really achieved was to live out my pain in a different location.

Proverbs 18:21 *"Death and life are in the power of the tongue, and those who love it will eat its fruit."*

I truly believe that what we declare about ourselves and about others has impact. Our responses to words spoken over us have the potential to define us, both for good and for bad. So, as I closed the door of the vehicle that would deliver me to my new and *'better life'*, you would think my thoughts would have been focused on adventure. Nope!

My head pounded with hurtful words and anger burned within my heart *"I'll give her 6 months and she will be into drugs and prostitution"*. Those were the last words I heard before I left the house that day and these careless words from someone I loved fuelled a deep bitterness within me. The same anger that drove me to prove them wrong also took its toll on me emotionally and by the time I had finished high school, I was a 47 kg time bomb of suppressed rage. I was the perfect clown... a smile to charm the world and a hidden tear concealed my pain.

And as I simmered those words took root in my soul, I allowed them to poison me. *No longer was anger a feeling I had but the person I had become.* I could see nothing beyond the hurt and it consumed me.

Who am I really?

By God's grace and through His eternal love for me, I am learning who I am and who I am in Him is not dependent on another person's opinion or even their reactions or responses to me. It doesn't even have anything to do with what I think of myself. What I have come to understand is that the ONLY opinion that counts is God's. What He says about us is often very different to what others say about us or even how we view ourselves.

The most valuable lesson

Have you ever been in a place where you want so much to reach out to people but are afraid of what that might mean? Well this was me a few years ago and for the first time in my life I found myself living alone in a house that echoed from the hollowness rather than the voices of children. My relationships were such that I would give enough to get what I needed but not so much that I felt vulnerable and uncomfortable. Fear ensured that I rarely committed to any social invitation but I made comments and excuses like *"I'll let you know"* or *"I'll see how I go"*.

I had made no real effort to engage or invite people into my life and so now when *'I needed them'* their own lives were full and their time stretched. In hindsight I thank God for this, even though at the time I felt hurt and forgotten.

Of all the things God has taught me, this I hold most precious...

- In a time when there was no one else to meet my need, *He was there*;
- When the nights were long and fraught with loneliness, *He held me in His arms and rocked me to sleep*;
- When the tears fell and there was no one to wipe them dry, *He caught them in a jar*;
- When my mind played games that questioned my self-worth, *He showed me who I was in Him*;
- When circumstances threatened to swamp my faith, *He guided me through and set me on dry ground*;
- When the cries of my heart fell on empty rooms, *He heard my prayers and filled the void with His love.*

POEM
You are my all

Oh Lord, I feel your gentle presence,
I know your hand upon my life,
I marvel at the miracles You are
performing within my very being.

When I am weak, Your awesome strength overwhelms me,
And yet... You take me gently into your bosom.
Your loving gentleness and compassion
revealing, binding and healing
my deepest wounds.

I praise You Lord for the joy that
consumes my soul, for the words of
encouragement You gently whisper
in my moments of despair.
Your Word satisfies me in my moment of hunger.

You are my towering fortress, a King worthy of praise,
A Father worthy of honour, A Husband worthy of love
and a Friend worthy of respect.

You are my all... You are the source of my fulfilment!
Felicity Eagan

As much as I love my children, my friends and my family, I have also learnt that they are not my source and that they will (without fail) let me down over and over and over again. Just as I will them. They are beautiful, wonderful, fabulous, gifted people but *they are not God* and are therefore subject to failure just as I am. My fulfilment comes only from God and He must be the foundation on which my identity and self-worth is built because it is only when He forms the cornerstone of my life, that everything else can fall into plumb. When His truth permeates our lives then out of a position of strength 'healthy' relationships, attitudes and perspectives are formed and nurtured.

The chosen Stone and His chosen people

1 Peter 2:4-6 "*Coming to Him as to a living stone, rejected indeed by men, but chosen by God and precious, you also, as living stones, are being built up a spiritual house, a holy priesthood, to offer up spiritual sacrifices acceptable to God through Jesus Christ. Therefore it is also contained in the Scripture, 'behold, I lay in Zion a chief cornerstone, elect, precious, and he who believes on Him will by no means be put to shame.'"*

A word of caution

Knowing who we are in God should not be used as a weapon to tear down others. Our mandate is still to love and show compassion. Jesus knew who He was and had confidence in His position, yet He never used this understanding to big-note Himself and make others feel inferior. Instead, He used His understanding as a platform from which to edify and encourage others.

A question for reflection

If all the people you loved and the things you counted on were taken away, would you be ok on your own, just you and God? Or would the very foundation of your world fall apart?

When you look in the mirror do you see the person of worth? Or has your self-worth been eroded and defined by careless words, popular opinion or the roles you play?

Who or what is your first love? Who comes first in your life?

The Bible says in **Matthew 19:24** that **"... it is easier for a camel to go through the eye of a needle than for a rich man to enter the kingdom of God."** Why? Because his riches were more important to him than God's call on his life.

Luke 12:34 "For where your treasure is, there your heart will be also."

If God allowed Satan to test you as He allowed Job to be tested in the book of Job and if everything on this earth that is precious to you is stripped away, would you also take that pain and declare **"The Lord gave and the Lord has taken away, blessed be the name of the Lord?" Job 1:21b**

The life and pain of Job challenges me beyond measure. I pray that even in the depths of such adversity I would turn my eyes in worship to Christ. Our hope is in Him.

News flash!

People will let you down! Your husband, your children, your family, your friends, your animals, your things, your investments, the government, social institutions and even

Felicity Eagan

the church will fail you at times. You cannot even place hope in yourself ... *even you will let you down!*

But if we shift our expectations and no longer look to people and 'things' to meet our needs and align ourselves with what God's Word says about us then we shall truly walk in His freedom and liberty.

We shall "***know the 'truth' and the 'truth' will set us free!" (see John 8:32)***

> *O soul, are you weary and troubled? No*
> *light in the darkness you see?*
> *There's light for a look at the Saviour,*
> *and life more abundant and free!*
> **(Verse 1 of the Hymn - Turn your eyes upon Jesus)**

182

WEEK 37

SOW WITH PRAYERS OF TEARS

Scripture of the week

Psalm 126:5-6 *"Those who sow in tears will reap in joy. He who continually goes forth weeping, bearing seed for sowing, shall doubtless come again with rejoicing, bringing his sheaves with him."*

Prayer of the week

Lord, use me I pray. Let me be a vessel that is willing. Willing to move as Your Spirit leads, willing to lay down myself for Your greater purpose. Instil in me a greater desire to seek Your heart. A desire to be more Christ-like in everything I do and say. Let me see the world through Your eyes. *'Break my heart for what breaks Yours'* and as I sow with prayers of tears, Lord, that You would prepare a plentiful harvest ready to be reaped with songs of joy. In Jesus name. **AMEN**

Thought of the week
Sow with prayers of tears

I couldn't sleep, I was deeply troubled and I had no real idea why. All I knew was that I urgently needed to pray for a friend but as I opened my mouth I found that there were no words just a deep sorrow and aching within which brought tears that streamed down my face and continued to flow for what seemed like hours until finally exhausted, I fell asleep.

I woke late the next morning and made myself coffee confused about what I had experienced the night before. As I sat down to study, the urgency and the burden came again, without warning and with equal intensity and I closed my books allowing the tears to run freely down my cheeks. I cried and I cried and then as quickly as they started, they stopped and I sat there wondering what just happened... *was I having a breakdown?*

I poured out my thoughts and fears to God in my journal, it was my way of making sense of it all. I found out several days later that at the very time I was moved to pray without words, just tears, my friend was in need. The Holy Spirit had used me to intercede on their behalf and though I didn't realise it at the time, those tears were Holy Spirit inspired prayers, each one of them the perfect intercession, not hindered by my words but aligned with the perfect will of God. I did not know exactly what I was praying for but He knew and each tear that fell sent up a silent plea to God that He might show mercy and act on behalf of one He loved.

Romans 8:26-27 *"Likewise the Spirit also helps in our weaknesses. For we do not know what we should pray for as we ought, but the Spirit Himself makes intercession for* *us with groanings which cannot be uttered. Now He who searches the hearts knows what the mind of the Spirit is, because He makes intercession for the saints according to the will of God."*

As God is softening my heart, I am finding myself moved to tears a lot lately not just for my friend but for injustice, for the living who are lost and dying without hope, for the complexity of a spiritually impoverished world whose priorities are warped and distorted and far from the heart of God. For a people group that have experience horrors that few of us will ever understand, a nation in desperate need and for which He has caused my heart to be 'carried away captive'.

Jeremiah 29:7 *"And seek the peace of the city where I have caused you to be carried away captive, and pray to the Lord for it; for in its peace you will have peace."*

As I have tried to understand what it is God requires of me as He leads me to pray, I begin to appreciate the implications of ***Psalm 51:17*** *"The sacrifices of God are a broken spirit, a broken and a contrite heart - These, O God, You will not despise."*

A willing vessel

God's desire for us is to imitate Christ and commit ourselves to Him with a heart of humility and repentance. All He requires of us is to sit at His feet and allow Him to work through us. It is His work we just need to be a willing vessel, willing to lay down our own rights, feelings, opinions, fears and insecurities. Willing to cast off our pre-conceived ideas of how and when and in what way we think He should work and just say *"God, I am willing, to do whatever it is Your Spirit prompts".*

I Peter 2:21-23 *"For to this you were called, because Christ also suffered for us, leaving us an example, that you should follow His steps: who committed no sin, nor was deceit found in His mouth; who, when He was reviled, did not revile in return; when He suffered, He did not threaten, but committed Himself to Him who judges righteously."*

Quote:

"I'm convinced that it is not our 'fullness' that attracts God, but our 'emptiness'. If you are willing to be used of God, and learn to be emptied of 'self', then God will use you."
(Joyce Scott)

WEEK 38

LOSING SIGHT OF THE DESTINATION

Scripture of the week

Psalm 61:2 *"From the end of the earth I will cry to you, when my heart is overwhelmed; lead me to the rock that is higher than I."*

Prayer of the week

Lord, it is so easy to become distracted and lose focus of the vision You have placed within my heart when the busyness of life and the frailty of my own body pit themselves against it. When delays and situations leave me questioning, I pray that You would impart to me the courage to press in and forward and be faithful to that which I have been called. Give me strength when my strength fails, show me the way when my sight fails and restore my passion for Your calling when the road becomes hard to navigate. In Jesus Name. **AMEN**

Thought of the week
Losing sight of the destination

Since placing these devotions on my heart, the Lord has been pretty faithful in providing me not only with the topic but also the content.

On one occasion however God had given me a title and no message, so I sat at my computer for nearly two hours with nothing but the title. I researched and read and found no inspiration. I was feeling tired and discouraged and I was on the verge of giving up on the message all together.

Eventually ideas started to slowly surface but it was like extracting teeth. Somehow I managed to get something on paper but even so, I was second guessing the words and felt hesitant, wondering if it was of God or just of me. This time, I just didn't feel God in the writing or the delivery.

All in all, I felt pretty crappy and discouraged, so much so that I was wondering if perhaps the season of devotionals had come to an end and that I had just missed God's memo. OOOOH that enemy is sneaky! He had me in a self-pity puddle as deep as the Grand Canyon and I couldn't see it for looking.

2 Corinthians 5:7 *"For we walk by faith, not by sight."*

In the form of His Word, God had provided me with a compass to successfully navigate my way to the destination He'd shown me. But when the path became shrouded in fog, I forgot to look at the compass and started focusing on the circumstances and as a result slipped down the embankment and into the mire of self-pity.

Had I of recognised the situation for what it truly was (nothing more than a blind spot in the road), I would have acknowledged my failure, allowed Him to lead me back to the path, re-entered the coordinates and headed off once again. Really, what I really needed to do when discouragement took hold was to press into God, take the focus off my insecurity (backwards pride) and re-focus it on the vision the Lord had given me.

Beauty for ashes

The words, *'beauty for ashes'* dropped into my mind as I drove through an area that was regenerating after the fires. I recognised the words as being significant and thought that perhaps God wanted me to write about this topic again. That evening when I got home I was reading my devotional and the verse that was highlighted was *'Beauty for Ashes'*. Later, propped up in bed, the words *'beauty for ashes'* were confirmed again in the book I was reading. These words, *'beauty for ashes'*, were brought to my awareness 3 times by three different sources. God had my attention!

With three references to *'beauty for ashes'*, one would think that the obvious subject for the next devotion would be *'Beauty for Ashes'* but it wasn't. Instead, the Lord has taught me something else from this experience.

That the journey is not always smooth and the path will not always be clear but we need to trust in His

system of navigation and not on what we see and hear and feel.

Our sense of direction is flawed and can cause us to lose our way when the road becomes foggy or we hit a blind corner, but His direction will always be true regardless of the circumstances. God took what I knew, the verse *'Beauty for Ashes'* and lead me to find a deeper truth in **Isaiah 61:1-3** which is in a nutshell the vision for these devotions.

At a time when I was discouraged and felt I was done, His Word encouraged me to continue. That even though I had encountered a blind corner and become disorientated, the course had not changed and *the journey was still valid.*

1 Corinthians 15:58 *"Therefore my beloved brethren, be steadfast, immovable, always abounding in the work of the Lord knowing that your labour is not in vain in the Lord."*

If God has placed a vision on your heart but you are struggling to see it come to fruition or your have lost your direction somewhere along the way, I pray that you would find the courage to wait on Him and trust Him. Revisit the scriptures and confirmations that He gave you and be encouraged by His Word for it is a *lamp unto thy feet.*

Regardless of which stage of the journey you find yourself, may you press on knowing that your efforts and labour are not in vain and may the Lord of the Harvest bless you abundantly!

"Wait on the Lord; be of good courage, and
He shall strengthen your heart; wait I say, on the Lord!'
Psalm 27:14

"And let us not grow weary while doing good,
for in due season we shall reap if we do not lose heart"
Galatians 6:9

GOD LOVES A CHEERFUL GIVER

Scripture of the week

1 Chronicles 29:9 *"Then the people rejoiced, for they had offered willingly, because with a loyal heart they had offered willingly to the Lord; and King David also rejoiced greatly."*

Prayer of the week

Father I thank You and praise You for the blessings You have given me. Show me each day how I might take these gifts and use them to show love and bless others. Teach me to operate out of a position of eternal abundance acknowledging always that the earth is Yours and the fullness thereof. Help me to diligently obey Your commands and walk uprightly in Your ways that I might know Your blessings forever. In Jesus name. **AMEN**

Thought of the week
God loves a cheerful giver!

Out of the mouth of babes!

Recently I was sitting in church and I had placed my offering in the bag watching silently as it made its way steadily towards the front row, its final destination!

Suddenly, the reverence was broken as a bundle of little legs pounded deliberately up the centre aisle, his eyes desperately focused on the steward ahead. His arm was outstretched before him and clutched in his chubby little hand was a ten dollar note which flapped wildly as his arms swung to and fro with the effort of running.

He flew past the pew I was sitting in and as he did so he cried out urgently...***"It's not too late!"***

I smiled as the steward stopped, turned and then stooped to allow the child to place his offering in the bag and I thought to myself *"If only we all brought our offerings to the Lord with such eager and unabashed willingness!"*

Later I realised that the real joy of that moment was found in the wisdom of the words that came from the mouth of a child..."*It's not too late.*"

2 Corinthians 9:6-7 *"But this I say; He who sows sparingly will also reap sparingly, and he who sows bountifully will also reap bountifully. So let each one give as he purposes in his heart, not grudgingly or of necessity; for God loves a cheerful giver."*

It wasn't that long ago that I had everything I could ever need and more and you know what? I was miserable! My mind was totally focussed on accumulating wealth and my house was filled with things I rarely used, much less needed. I was bogged down by debt and financial juggling and I operated from a position of a 'poverty mentality' or perceived lack rather than a position of abundance. Nothing, no matter how much I had, was ever enough. *The more I had, the more I wanted.*

Quote:
*"2 Corinthians 9:5 teaches that giving should
NOT be an attitude of how much can
I KEEP, but how much can I GIVE."*
(Cooper P. Abrams)

This was me, when and if I gave it was always in consideration of my own needs first. I used to think it was being responsible but now I realise that it was nothing more than a distinct lack of faith in God and His provision for my life.

Romans 14:23 *"But he who doubts is condemned if he eats, because he does not eat from faith; for whatever is not from faith is sin."* Ouch!

For me, losing everything broke the yoke. The bondage of *'having things'* no longer held any power over me and as I determined to give even out of my lack, God provided the seed I needed to further sow into the lives of others. I cannot describe the miracle that occurred within the depths of my heart, only that there was a joy in *'giving'* that I had never found in *'getting'*.

And giving is not just about money, it is not just about paying tithes or giving monetary offerings although these things might reflect the shift in attitude that comes from the heart. It is the revelation that *"the earth is the Lord's and the fullness thereof..."* that placed me in a position of eternal abundance and released me to give freely and without reservation.

Psalm 24:1 goes on to say that everything in it (*'its fullness'*), including you belongs to the Lord. This means that your gifts, your talents your time and your 'things', everything you have and everything you *are* belongs to God and so, in the light of this, the act of offering goes well beyond money.

God desires for us to give willingly and joyfully, not only of our finances but of ourselves. And as we faithfully use that which He has given us, He will replenish it and multiply it that we might be a cup running over, blessed by the Lord to be a blessing to others in everything we do and have.

"It's not too late" to bring your offering to the Lord.

May you find opportunities to take that which God has blessed you with and use it to bless others.

> *"I beseech you therefore, brethren, by the mercies of God,*
> *that you present your bodies a living*
> *sacrifice, holy acceptable*
> *to God, which is your reasonable service."*
> ***Romans 12:1***

WEEK 40

SYNERGY–WORKING TOGETHER!

Scripture of the week

John 17:23 *"I in them, and You in Me; that they may be made perfect in one, and that the world may know that You have sent Me, and have loved them as You have loved Me."* (The words of Jesus).

Prayer of the week

Father, I pray that you reveal to me the gifts that are within me. Give me the courage to take those gifts and by faith use them to build up and edify those around me that Your church might operate in the fullness of unity as You originally intended. Meld us as believers together as one unit Lord, powered by Your Spirit and inspired to action by the knowledge and conviction of Truth according to Your Word. In Jesus name. **AMEN**

Thought of the week
Synergy–working together!

I work for a company who, among other things manufactures rubber matting and our 'hero' product is a mat specifically designed to protect livestock from slipping and falling.

I have spent quite a bit of time getting to know this mat and I can now say I am on a first names basis with it. Why? Because it is my job to promote it and to do this effectively, I have to know it intimately.

I have been commissioned by my boss to help people understand the implicit value of the mat and to convey why it is superior to the cheap replica they can buy from any hardware store. My efforts educate the market and plant a seed of desire in the minds of potential buyers.

One of the salesmen in our office, who I will refer to as 'The Guru', also has a deep relationship with the product and is unwaveringly convinced that it holds the answer to so many of the problems he sees out in the field. His conviction compels him to share the substantial benefits of this 'treasure' with those in need and his enthusiasm alone is a huge accolade to its worth which often brings them to a point of purchase.

On the face of it, this 'product' is just a mat. Few people are aware of its hidden benefits and its ability to positively impact the health and wellbeing of the creatures it was designed for. But, it cannot sell itself! It requires a team of people to promote it and spread its good news to those who need it but who just don't know it yet.

People like me (the sower of ideas) and 'The Guru' (skilled in bringing people to a point of decision), along with a myriad of other people (each one doing their part) all form part of a team through which every mat sale is made. Individually, we might sell a few but probably not very many. Collectively however, (and working under the Boss's guidance) we are a formidable team and the sales figures reflect this.

Ok, so you are probably sitting there right now thinking, what a lovely story? **And** your point is?

Well, there is actually two **'Ands'** to this story. The first relates to...

The power of Synergy

The word 'Synergy' comes from the Greek word *'sunergos'* or working together. It is defined as: *"The interaction or cooperation of two or more organisations, substances, or other agents to produce a combined effect greater than the sum of their separate effects"*. In other words, when two or more people combine their efforts the results are greater than if one was to try and do it on their own.

The above illustration highlights the power of synergy in the process of selling. As a combined unit we sell a huge amount of mats, far more than any one of us could sell on our own. This is because each of us has a unique skill that we bring to the table. Others might also be able to perform our job to a degree but they rarely have the same capacity as the person who is gifted in that area. The Guru for example is a born salesperson. He is personable and friendly and has the ability to make people feel at ease. He calls his clients 'his friends' and he treats them as such. His ability to maintain good customer relationships astounds me. He on the other hand thinks what I do is amazing and cannot fathom why I cringe at the very thought of trying to sell anything to anyone–I even hate talking on the telephone! I can turn my hand to accounts but it is not my strength and I don't enjoy them. The accounts girl on the other hand is a whizz with figures and seems to juggle multiple tasks and calculations with ease, taking everything in her stride. I often tell her I wouldn't have her job for quids, yet she is in her element!

Our Boss is very wise indeed! The right people for the right jobs and the results are powerful!

God is the author of Synergy

Romans 12:4-5 *"For as we having many members in one body, but all the members do not have the same function, so we being many, are one body in Christ, and individually members of one another."* (synergy).

As a church, this principle of synergy is also very powerful. It is when each person in the body discovers their God given gifts and abilities and begins to operate in them that the church becomes more effective in reaching the unsaved for Christ. When we try to fill shoes that we were never meant to wear, we find ourselves frustrated and unfulfilled. Our gifts and callings compliment the way God wired us and when we operate within them as

God intended they are not burdensome but bring great satisfaction and joy.

Romans 12:6 *"Having then gifts differing according to the grace that is given to us, let us use them: ... if prophecy, let us prophesy in proportion to our faith"...* **(also read v 7-8)**

But more than this they bring a level of unity and effectiveness to the church that cannot be found otherwise. And when you couple this with the awesome power and wisdom of our God (The Boss) you have a formidable team of believers who are fully equipped to undertake the Lords commission, t*o proclaim the gospel; to make disciples and; to love in a way we never knew possible.*

The second **'And'** is about the mat itself. Huh you say?

As I was writing this I realised that this story is like a parable and that the 'mat' is a bit like the Bible. On the face of it, the Bible is just a book... Few people are aware of its hidden benefits and its ability to positively impact the health and wellbeing of the creatures it was designed for. It cannot sell itself, it needs a team of people to promote it and spread its good news to those who need it but just don't know it yet. Our conviction should compel us to use our gifts to convey the significant benefits of this 'treasure' to those in need and our enthusiasm alone should be a huge accolade to it's worth, inspiring others to the point of decision.

So many people are searching for answers to life's questions. They are looking for purpose and fulfilment in pagan religions and self-enlightenment never realising that that the emptiness that are feeling can only be filled by God (Yaweh) and that cheap replicas will inevitably end in disappointment. The Bible was inspired by God for the purpose of changing lives. It holds within its pages the answer to so many of the issues that people struggle with today.

God has chosen us to spread His message of salvation. He has equipped us with gifts that, when used together to serve one another form a balanced and effective team, *perfectly synergised to bring hope to the lost.*

"And He Himself gave some to be apostles, some prophets, some evangelists, and some pastors and teachers, for the equipping of the saints and for the work of the ministry for the edifying of the body of Christ, till we all come to the unity of the faith and of the knowledge of the Son of God, to a perfect man, to the measure of the stature of the fullness of Christ."
Ephesians 4:11-13

WEEK 41

WHERE DOES YOUR HOPE LIE?

Scripture of the week

Jeremiah 17:5-8 *"Thus says the Lord: "Cursed is the man who trusts in man and makes flesh his strength, whose heart departs from the Lord. For he shall be like a shrub in the desert, and shall not see when good comes, but shall inhabit the parched places in the wilderness, in a salt land which is not inhabited.*

"Blessed is the man who trusts in the Lord, and whose hope is the Lord. For he shall be like a tree planted by the waters, which spreads out its roots by the river, and will not fear when heat comes; but its leaf will be green, and will not be anxious in the year of drought, nor will cease from yielding fruit."

Prayer of the week

Lord, Thank You that You are my source, my Provider. That You have not given me a spirit of fear that I should be swayed by the circumstances going on around me, but instead a sound mind, constant in the knowledge that You are faithful and will meet my every need just as You promised. Your provision will be perfect for every situation and in You, I shall not want. **AMEN**

Thought of the week
Where does your hope lie?

There I was sitting at the computer and eavesdropping on the news filtering in from the next room, the topic? The Federal Budget!

STOP! Before you turn the page, HEAR ME OUT! My intention is not to bore you with a run-down on my political viewpoints, but the budget was definitely the channel through which this message came into existence.

In preparation for ministry, I was about to return to full-time study. Financially that meant that I would *'voluntarily'* position myself within the lowest income bracket and so immediately my mind began to swim with the potential burdens that this new budget would bring on me personally.

The news reader's words echoed in my brain and I felt a growing sense of fear and uncertainty about the future. My life experiences caused me to respond negatively and with a short-sighted, knee jerk reaction. As I felt the panic rise, I heard God speak. *"Who is your source?"*

Four words, that's all it took. By a single, gentle reprimand, the chains of fear were broken and suitably chastised. I quietly replied, *"You are, Lord."* In that moment of danger I heard my Shepherd's voice and I felt His rod of correction nudge me back to safety.

How awesome! How wise! How patient and how gracious is our God!

1 Peter 5:8 *"Be sober, be vigilant; because your adversary the Devil walks about like a roaring lion, seeking whom he may devour."*

How important is it to be attentive and clear-headed?

It is a matter of life and death. Why? Because...

- In a fleeting moment of inattention, *I had forgotten who I was.*
- In a fleeting moment of inattention, *I opened the door to my old fear nature.*
- In a fleeting moment of inattention, *I came so close to letting the Devil devour my joy.*

A shift in perspective

The Bible tells us in **Psalm 146:3** *"Do not put your trust in princes, nor in a son of man* (son of Adam), *in whom there is no help."*

When we get a grip on the fact that God, the Creator of Heaven and Earth is our source it totally changes the way we look at things like the Federal Budget, our jobs and our incomes. We have confidence that God will provide even when the circumstances of our lives point to lack. As children of God, we no longer need to be imprisoned by the negative emotions that come with fear but instead we stand constant and secure in the knowledge that God will meet us in our time of need just as He did the widow in *1 Kings 17:13-16.* Her circumstances said, *"you and your son shall die from starvation"* but God said, ***"your jar of flour will not be spent, nor your jug of oil empty."***

So, if you are feeling dismayed by your current financial situation and can only see the negative impact that it threatens to impose on your life, I urge you to look up. If you are His child, then know this, *'He'* (not the Government, not the budget, not your job, not your impending inheritance or investment) *is your source.* When we give up our tendency to rely on the systems of this world we give God room to perform miracles in every area of our lives.

So, be alert!

Don't give room for the enemy to gain a foothold in your life. Remind yourself daily *"God is my source, in Him will I trust!"*

Psalm 118:8 *"It is better to trust in <u>the Lord</u> than to put confidence in man."*

Incidentally, ponder this... Did you know that *Psalm 118:8* is the verse at the very middle of the King James Bible and that the words, *'The Lord'* are what lies at the very centre?

Remember...

> *"Blessed is the man who trusts in the LORD, and whose hope is the Lord."*
> **Jeremiah 17:7**

for...

> *"The Lord is my portion, says my soul, therefore, I hope in Him!"*
> **Lamentations 3:24**

WEEK 42

THE PARABLE OF
THE LOST SHEEP

Scripture of the week

Matthew 18:11 *"For the Son of Man has come to save that which was lost."*

Prayer of the week

Lord, open my understanding that I might comprehend the hidden truths found within Your words and parables. Convict my heart that I might dwell in a continuous state of both humility and repentance. Remind me that wisdom is not directly correlated to how long I have walked beside You, but how much I have allowed You to work within me. Help me to acknowledge the reality of my own weakness. In Jesus Name. **AMEN**

Thought of the week
Searching for the stray

I have been pondering on the verses found in **Matthew 18:10-14** and **Luke 15:4-7** which talk about the parable of the lost sheep.

I have found myself wondering each time what point Jesus was trying to make in this parable. To me it doesn't make sense to leave 99 sheep out in the wilderness in order to search out a single sheep that has run amok.

In the context of today's business acumen what Jesus was proposing would be seen as absurd. Who, in their right mind would put the majority at risk for the sake of a minority? It could potentially mean financial ruin.

Society often takes the stance that some things need to be sacrificed for the greater good. Jesus on the other hand is effectively declaring the exact opposite and when Jesus uses a parable to teach you can be sure that there is generally a hidden truth well worth uncovering, *perhaps the seemingly insignificant matters more than we know.*

And perhaps this parable holds both a story of redemption for the one that was lost and a parallel warning to the 'just' Pharisees against a haughty spirit which left them believe they were righteous and 'beyond' the need for a repentant heart.

Luke 15:4-7 *"What man of you, having an hundred sheep, if he lose one of them, doth not leave the ninety and nine in the wilderness, and go after that which is lost, until he find it? And when he hath found it, he layeth it on his shoulders, rejoicing. And when he cometh home, he calleth together his friends and neighbours, saying unto them, rejoice with me; for I have found my sheep which was lost. I say unto you, that likewise joy shall be in heaven over one sinner that repenteth, more than over ninety and nine just persons, which need no repentance."*

A story of redemption

Is Jesus saying that the 99 are less important than the one? I think not! But neither is He saying that they are more important. To Jesus, each individual is as important as another. The flock may or may not encounter danger in the Shepherds absence but to ignore the plight of the one lost sheep would almost certainly mean its demise and the loss to the Shepherd would be so much deeper than mere stock value.

In Jesus day, a good shepherd knew his flock intimately. He would have known their individual markings and he would have known their unique personalities and temperaments. Each of those sheep would also have known the inflections and intonations of the shepherd's voice, the sound of his footsteps and of his breathing, the scent of his perspiration.

The bond between the Shepherd and his sheep was hallmarked by a deep trust, reliance and affection. The shepherd knew his sheep by name and his sheep responded to his leading.

Now, sheep are not known for their sensibility, *in fact sheep are pretty dumb and unpredictable*!

I have owned a few sheep in my time and if you have ever tried to round them up on your own, you are in for a wild and erratic chase. (Perhaps I should have spent a bit more time at Shepherd School!)

A lone sheep in the wilderness would be a prime target for predators. It is unable to provide for itself or protect itself and it will wander aimlessly, incapable of even seeking out a water source. Without the guidance and protection of the shepherd it will eventually die either from predator attack, dehydration or sheer exhaustion.

Lost

One night my son did not get off the bus from school. I phoned the school thinking he had missed the bus, but he could not been found in the school ground. I phoned his friends parents hoping that perhaps someone had offered to give him a lift home but no one had. I drove the road from his school to home but he was not to be found and as darkness loomed closer, I felt myself brink on the edge of panic and hysteria as I began to fear for his safety.

A search party went out and after several hours I found him, exhausted, distressed and sitting crying on the side of a remote dirt road between his school and home. He had missed the bus and foolishly decided to walk, taking a wrong turn which resulted in him becoming lost. Now, I have other children which I also love dearly and focusing my full attention on finding the one who had become lost was in no way an indication that I loved them any less. In fact, if any one of them had of been lost my reaction would have been the same. The difference was that I knew that they were safe at home and in no immediate danger. Whilst I love my other children dearly, my primary concern at that moment was for my child that was lost.

When my son was found I cried for sheer relief that he was restored to me and safe and in my arms. I would never have stopped searching. This is the love of a mother... it is also the heart of a shepherd.

My son learnt a great lesson from this experience and the expression on his sobbing face as he ran into my arms spoke volumes to my heart. He was truly sorry for his condition. There is much rejoicing when one who is lost becomes found.

> *"Likewise, I say to you, there is joy in the presence of the angels of God over one sinner who repents."*
> **Luke 15:10**

WEEK 43

OUT OF THE DEPTHS OF GRIEF, GRACE ABOUNDS

Scripture of the week

1 Peter 5:10 *"But may the God of all grace, who called us to His eternal glory by Christ Jesus, after you have suffered a while, perfect, establish, strengthen and settle you."*

Prayer of the week

Lord, help me to remember to thank and praise You in all things, knowing that in every situation You are there comforting and guiding me by Your Spirit. I pray that Your hope might abound in my soul and that I will seek Your face with earnest. May my cup overflow with Your joy and peace that I might provide comfort also to those who despair. **AMEN**

Thought of the week
Out of the depths of grief, grace abounds

"When you pass through the waters I will be with You
and the river will not overflow you.
When you walk through
the fire you shall not be burned, nor
will the flame scorch you."
Isaiah 43:2

I saw my dad for his 86th birthday. It was the first time in around 10 years we had spoken. The joy on his face when I walked in the room will remain with me forever and the hurts we had harboured for so long seemed to fade into insignificance as forgiveness bridged the gap that had separated us. My dad died a week later.

I sat by his hospital bed grief stricken and as he faded in and out of consciousness I sang *"Jesus loves me"*. He was a man of music and I pray he heard my song. As he took his final breath he turned to me and in a moment of clarity looked into my eyes and grasped my hand tightly and through the pain that streaked his face I saw in his eyes a silent recognition of love for his little girl lost who had finally come home.

In the midst of sadness I witnessed the grace of God abound in so many ways. Not only was I given the opportunity to let him know I loved him and to say goodbye but my Dad's passing brought reconciliation and healing to others also.

Proverbs 15:23 *"A man has joy by the answer of his mouth, and a word spoken in due season, how good it is!"*

The kindness of a stranger

That same evening a complete stranger bestowed one of the most precious acts of selfless compassion upon us, even though at the time we did not fully understand the significance of her kindness. The tea lady at the hospital served us coffee as we waited for our older sister to arrive from interstate. A couple of hours later she returned and brought us a hamper of drinks and food. Afterwards we realised that she, having finished her shift, had gone to the supermarket and purchased the items and returned to deliver them to us. We were so humbled by her act of kindness and consideration that we brought her a card and a small thank you gift, a rose candle. We watched the tears well in her eyes as she opened it and joined our own tears with hers as she told us that she had buried her own mother only the week before, the rose candle was her mother's favourite scent.

God knows and cares and uses us to bless others, even in times of despair.

Lord, may my cup overflow with Your joy and peace that I might provide comfort also to those who despair.

How great is our God!

WEEK 44

LOVE THEM LIKE JESUS

Scripture of the week

Jeremiah 8:21-22 "*For the hurt of the daughter of my people I am hurt. I am mourning; astonishment has taken hold of me. Is there no balm in Gilead, is there no physician there? Why then is there no recovery for the health of the daughter of my people?*"

Prayer of the week

Lord, give me the courage to see the pain that is all too easy to ignore. Give me willingness to extend Your arm of love to those who so desperately need it. May I be Your hands and Your feet. May I be a voice crying in the wilderness. May I be girded with Your truth and my feet be shod with Your gospel of peace. May I take up the breastplate of righteousness, the shield of faith and the sword of the Spirit and may I place on my head the helmet of salvation. Lord, teach me to pray in Spirit and in truth that I may open my mouth boldly to make known the mystery of the gospel. In Jesus name. **AMEN**

Thought of the week
Love them like Jesus

What do you say to someone when there doesn't seem to be any words that fit? How can you bring hope when their situation screams hopeless? How do you counsel when things just don't add up and there seems to be more questions than answers? What do you say to someone who has lost their best friend? How do you bring hope to someone who is fighting for their life? How do you ease the pain of those suffering grief and loss? How do you minister to hearts that are battered by life's storms? I have found myself recently asking these questions and the words of a song by **Casting Crowns** keep coming back to me each time. *"Love them like Jesus."*

So what exactly does that mean? To love like Jesus?

When I look at the scriptures, this is what I get. First of all we need to be '**WILLING**'—*willing* to move out of our comfort zone; *willing* to place the needs of others before our own; *willing* to be involved the lives of those who are struggling and; *willing* to rise above our insecurities, our preconceived ideas, our weakness, our vanity, our fears and our pride for the higher call of God—even *willing to touch the untouchable.*

Matthew 8:2-3 *"And behold, a leper came and worshiped Him, saying, Lord if You are willing, You can make me clean. Then Jesus put out His hand and touched him, saying, I am willing, be cleansed."*

We need to be **'Willing to Serve'** and *sometimes this comes at great personal cost*. Jesus said in **Luke 22:27** that He was among the people as **'One who serves'** and he came humbly before His fellow man as a servant. If Christ would willingly humble Himself to serve the lost and broken hearted, how much more should we be willing to serve?

Mark 10:45 *"For even the Son of Man did not come to be served, but to serve, and to give His life a ransom for many."*

We need to be **'Willing to be Love in Action'**. *Words are not enough.* What you do often speaks louder than what you say. Love is practical... *it takes a homeless man to breakfast.*

I was driving to work early one morning. It was freezing. As I passed the park shelter I glanced across to see a homeless man lying curled up on the cold hard bench. My heart bunched up and I felt the Spirit's call but as I glanced at my watch I kept going as I was going to be late. By the time I got to work I felt miserable, where were my priorities? I look for that man every morning now. I pray that the Lord will allow Him to cross my path again. He hasn't. I missed an opportunity to love like Jesus and I am so certain that His choice in that situation would have been so different to mine. I pray that by His grace I will choose better next time. If Christ showed love in action in everything He did and every situation He encountered, how much more should we be willing to show love in action?

1 John 3:18 *"My little children, let us not love in word or in tongue, but in deed and in truth."*

We need to be **'Willing to Forgive'**, *even when you suffer persecution.* Jesus said in **Luke 23:24** even as the crowds were crying out to crucify Him *"Father forgive them, for they know not what they do."* If Christ would cry out for mercy for the very people that would take His life, how much more should we be willing to forgive?

Matthew 5:44 *"But I say to you, love your enemies, bless those who curse you, do good to those who hate you, and pray for those who spitefully use you and persecute you."*

We need to be **'Willing to Give'** of *our time, of our finances, our abilities and our emotions.* There are numerous instances in the Bible where Jesus met the needs of both individuals and the multitudes. He fed them physically and spiritually, both with bread and water and the bread and water of life. He prayed for the sick, He cleansed the unclean and He delivered those who were possessed.

The verses of **Matthew 14: 12-23** speak loudly to me of the extent of Jesus compassion and love. In **verse 12**-He receives word that His beloved friend John the Baptist has been beheaded. Such grief He would have known. In **verse 13** He tried to find a place on his own most likely to grieve but in **verse 14**, He is moved by compassion for the multitudes and ministers to their needs instead.

By the end of the day, He must have been exhausted and the disciples wanted to send the multitudes away but Jesus said *"Bring them here to me"* and He fed them. It was only then, when the needs of others had been met, that He took time out and went to the mountains to pray.

Jesus not only gave everything He had but everything He didn't have. He gave out of His weakness for the sake of love and only then renewed His strength in communion with His Father. Did He go for a nanna nap or to veg out in front of the TV? No! His priority when he was exhausted was to seek His Fathers face. Wow, perhaps there is a lesson to be learned in this verse alone.

If Christ would give with such relentless love and compassion, how much more should we be willing to give beyond our comfort zones?

Matthew 10:8 *"Heal the sick, cleanse the lepers, raise the dead, cast out demons. Freely you have received, freely give."*

We need to be **'Willing to stand for Truth'** The Lord once said to me during one of my journaling sessions, *"Fee, hard truths must be delivered with grace"* and when I look at His Word I can see that Jesus did just this. He used parables, He used words of knowledge (the woman at the well) He used scripture and He even used the very words of His accusers against themselves with grace. He preached an absolute gospel without excuse or compromise. He delivered it undefiled to all those who had 'ears to listen' because He knew that it was the undefiled Truth of the gospel that would set them free.

If Christ would give His life for the sake of the gospel, how much more should we be willing to deliver it with uncompromising integrity?

John 14:6 *"Jesus said I AM THE WAY, The Truth and The Life. NO ONE comes to the Father except through me."* (Emphasis mine).

Are you the salt of the Earth that Christ has called you to be? Do you add flavour to the lives of those who are hurting or as I did, do you divert your eyes and walk the other way because loves call is not convenient or, your discomfort and their need is too great and you feel inadequate? There is going to be times when you just don't have the answers and some things will never be known until we reach glory but you can show compassion, you can be an ear that listens, a shoulder to lean on and a hand to hold. You are His hands, His voice, His feet and in the act of loving, they will see Jesus and you will be a visible emblem of the hope that can be found in Him.

John 3:16 *"For God so loved that world, that he gave His only begotten Son, that whosoever believes in Him, shall not perish but have everlasting life."*

"Love them like Jesus, carry them to Him..."
(words from the Song 'Love them like Jesus' by Casting Crowns)

WEEK 45

YOU WANT ME TO DO WHAT?

Scripture of the week

John 13:3-5 *"Jesus, knowing that the Father had given all things into His hands, and that He had come from God and was going to God, rose from supper and laid aside His garments, took a towel and girded Himself. After that, He poured water into a basin and began to wash the disciples' feet, and to wipe them with the towel with which He was girded."*

Prayer of the week

Lord forgive me for my selfishness and self-righteous attitudes. Grant me grace to lay down my own rights that my life would be a witness to Your glory and transforming power. May it no longer be me that liveth but You that liveth in me. May the work You are doing in my heart be reflected in my actions, attitudes and responses. Grant me the courage to move against the tide, to travel the lesser road and to respond with a kingdom focus and Christ-like grace. In Jesus Name. **AMEN**

Thought of the week
You want me to do WHAT ???

I hate it when I so desperately want to get on my soap box in a fit of self-righteousness indignation and God tells me that, *I need to 'wash feet'!*

The lowest of the household servants washed feet, yet this is the model Christ gave us to follow. Jesus effectively said if we aspire to be great in the kingdom, we need to *'learn to wash feet'.*

Matthew 20:26 *"Yet it shall not be so among you; but whoever desires to become great among you, let him be your servant."*

So I said... *"Lord, in one breath you tell me I am a warrior princess and in the next, I am to wash feet? What sort of 'king's kid' washes feet?"* And He answered me, *"the sort of 'king's kid' that esteems the purposes of her Father's kingdom greater than her own".*

You know what? By the world's standards I might just be justified in my feelings. I may even have been *'right'*—but God has asked me to choose to forego my own rights to esteem another greater. In other words, He wants me to humbly serve them regardless of their response to me! *Grrrr...* I have to admit that to my sinful nature the very thought of submitting to this sort of humility drags against the grain.

But who am I to argue with God? So, in *'foot dragging'* obedience, I 'grudgingly' conceded and I got down on my knees and washed those dirty, smelly, festy feet that were calloused with corns and bunions and which I found so offensive. Why? Because I love Him, because He asked me to and because, He set His example before me.

I am pretty certain that Jesus didn't enjoy the prospect of carrying the heavy wooden cross His Father asked Him to carry any more than I enjoy humbling myself to wash feet. In fact, in **Luke 22:42**, Jesus actually prayed **"Father, if You are willing, take this cup from Me; yet, NOT MY WILL, but Yours be done."** In yet another perfect example, He rose above His fear and human nature and acted not only in obedience, but in love and compassion for the greater purpose of His Father's kingdom.

Where would we be today if Jesus our King did not humble Himself to the Father's will even unto death? Don't be deceived, there will be those God causes to cross our paths to who a single act of humility and compassion on our part could mean the difference between eternal life or damnation.

It starts with an act of obedience

So, as I ruthlessly grabbed hold of my will (groaning loudly as I did so) and brought it into submission, a strange and miraculous thing happened. The perceived importance of my own needs faded and my focus became single-mindedly fixed on bearing the foot washing cross that was now firmly strapped to my back and without even realising it my attitude begin to subtly shift. As I determined in my heart to follow His lead, my will and my actions naturally fell into step with His.

Increasingly, I am beginning to see my 'self-righteous responses' in the light of His greater purpose and they appear as filthy rags. By His grace I pray that my 'grudging' attitude becomes transformed into genuine willingness and compassion.

Luke 9:23 instructs us to **"take up our cross _daily_"** and I am realising that it requires a conscious and determined choice to do this, but it is also an imperative component of my faith if I am to convey His message of love and hope to those He places in my path with any real validity and conviction. So, as I make my way each day a little further towards that hill on which I will finally die to self, each step forward is a powerful witness to his sustaining grace in my life. For He makes it possible to carry that cross with joy and endurance and with each step I know that He has gone before me.

Unless we are willing to share in His suffering, then we will by no means share in His Glory. *(See Romans 8:17). And sometimes this means you are going to need to wash feet.*

Do you confound people with acts of mercy and compassion even when they don't deserve it, or do you harden your heart towards them, unwilling to back down on the basis that in your eyes they are wrong and you are right? Are you willing to give up you rights and respond with Christ-like love? Are you willing to change your focus from the internal perspective of your own rights and needs to the eternal perspective of the cross?

The road less travelled

Choosing to take up your cross takes courage, dedication and daily commitment but I believe it is only when we are willing to humble ourselves that we will truly be able to walk in the fullness of His purpose for our lives, and I am guessing that *regardless of the perceived status of this calling, its foundation will be found in the act of washing feet.*

> *"I have been crucified with Christ and I no longer live,*
> *but Christ lives in me. The life I now live in the body,*
> *I live by faith in the Son of God, who loved*
> *me and gave himself for me."*
> **Galatians 2:20**

WEEK 46

INTEGRITY

Scripture of the week

Ephesians 6:14 *"Stand firm therefore, having girded your waist with truth, having put on the breastplate of righteousness."*

Prayer of the week

Lord, let my words be backed up by love in action, let love in action be underpinned by Love Incarnate. Immerse me in Your truth Lord, that moving forward my life might be a model of steadfast integrity to the generations that watch my walk. In Jesus Name. **AMEN**

Thought of the week

Quote:
"Integrity is doing the right thing,
even if nobody is watching."
(Anonymous)

Integrity... we are told to have it but what is it exactly?

In the Encarta World Dictionary integrity is defined as follows: **Possession of firm principles:** *the quality of possessing and steadfastly adhering to high moral principles* or *professional standards.* **Completeness:** *the state of being complete or undivided.* **Wholeness:** *the state of being sound or undamaged.*

Possession of firm principles, completeness and wholeness

I have had the privilege of meeting some really lovely, well mannered, respectful and caring people, who are true to their word and are reliable and fair. People I would have no trouble leaving my children with or entrusting with my money or my heart. Sadly, I have also encountered some fairly dodgy individuals who say one thing and do another and who have bled me dry for everything they could get out of me without a single ounce of compassion, remorse or consideration.

I believe the point of difference lies in one word-*'integrity'*

People of integrity cannot be identified by looking at them, only by 'experiencing' them. A person's integrity starts with what they say but finishes in what they do and is underpinned by what they believe.

Blessed by a stranger

It was raining and I got out of my car to go into a shop. I would have been in the store for at least 20-30 minutes before returning to my car. As I went to get into my car a man in the next car knocked on his window to get my attention. He was a scruffy, unshaved individual who was missing several teeth and when he spoke it was obvious that he was not overly educated. He pointed to my car and asked me *"S'that yours?"* I looked at him curiously and said yes wondering why he was asking and as I stood there he reached back into his car, picked something up and then reached his hand out to give it to me.

Proverbs 28:6 *"Better is the poor who walks in his integrity than one perverse in his ways, though he be rich."*

When I hastily left my car 30 minutes earlier I had dropped my mobile phone on the ground outside my door. This man had found my phone and not only returned it to me but took the time to dry it from the rain and then waited almost half an hour for me to return to my car. I had wrongly misjudged his interest in my car and I was deeply humbled.

What makes one person return a phone and another pocket it? I believe it stems from the internal foundations of what you believe to be valuable.

Now, I am not for a minute suggesting that being financially poor translates to moral bankruptcy (in fact the opposite is often the case), but increasingly it is those deprived of moral and spiritual richness that are making news headlines for acts of crime, depravity, cruelty and malice.

We live in a world rampant in technology and it is becoming progressively common for children to grow up sitting in front of the television or computer, indiscriminately feeding their internal guidance systems with graphic acts of violence and self-gratification.

They are seen but not heard and much less spoken to or guided with firm boundaries and loving kindness. They learn to get what they can get, when they can get it, without concern or compassion for other human beings, even those within their own families. They are growing up devoid of Godly morals and firmly grounded principles and they live on the scraps of brokenness, rarely finding any sense of wholeness or completeness for the whole of their lives.

Matthew 24:35 *"Heaven and Earth will pass away but my words will by no means pass away."*

We shake our heads in disbelief when we hear of mass killings and crimes of human atrocity yet the Bible, often scorned for being redundant and outdated, describes in great detail such events *(Matthew 24)*. Why then are we surprised to find that *we do actually reap what we sow* even into the next generation?

The Bible says in *Proverbs 22:6* *"Train up a child in the way he should go, and when he is old he will not depart from it."* We often refer to this scripture in matters of building them up in the faith from an early age. But I think this principle runs deeper and applies to more than just faith. It is teaching them in such a way that they learn to internalise and value Godly morals and

Biblical principles so that when the rubber hits the road and they are faced with the 'tough' choices they remain undivided and unshaken in their beliefs. They don't crumble under the weight of popular opinion but hold firm to their convictions even when it means it will cost them personally.

Monkey see, monkey do

Proverbs 20:7 *"The righteous man walks in his integrity; His children are blessed after him."*

For most children the saying *'monkey see, monkey do'* holds true, they will imitate what you model and internalise both what you vocalise and what you do. If you say one thing but do something different, they learn that double standards are ok. If you diligently model good financial and work ethics—your children will learn the value of hard work, the principals of sowing and of the importance of being a good steward. If you love others as you love yourself (both openly and behind closed doors), your children learn to love. If you humble yourself to serve others, your children will learn to give selflessly with humility and compassion. If you live a life of faith, they will learn that God is faithful.

Some of these things I did well as a parent, many I did poorly. But fortunately for me this is not a message aimed at bringing to light my failings but more an encouragement to embrace the grace of God in our lives, allowing Him to strengthen us so that we can rise up as models of integrity to the younger generations.

When we model integrity, our children are blessed because they become apprentices who learn to walk also in the principles of integrity... *monkey see, monkey do.*

So I guess in layman's terms, integrity from a Biblical perspective could otherwise be defined as **'saying what you mean'**, **'meaning what you say'**, and **'doing what you say'**—all springing out of a heart immersed in Divine Truth.

> *"Keep your heart with all diligence, for*
> *out of it spring the issues of life.*
> *Put away from you a deceitful mouth,*
> *and put perverse lips far from you.*
> *Let your eyes look straight ahead, and*
> *your eyelids look right before you.*
> *Ponder the path of your feet, and let*
> *all your ways be established.*
> *Do not turn to the right or the left;*
> *remove your foot from evil."*
> **Proverbs 4:23-27**

WEEK 47

I WILL MEET YOU IN THE DARKNESS

Scripture of the week

Exodus 20:18-21 *"Now all the people witnessed the thunderings, the lightning flashes, the sound of the trumpet, and the mountain smoking; and when the people saw it, they trembled and stood afar off. Then they said to Moses, "You speak with us, and we will hear; but let not God speak with us, lest we die."*

And Moses said to the people, "Do not fear; for God has come to test you, and that His fear may be before you, so that you may not sin."

So the people stood afar off, but Moses drew near the thick darkness where God was."

Prayer of the week

Father I trust You. Yea thou I walk in the valley of the shadow of death I will fear no evil. For You are with me (even in the thick darkness). Your rod and Your staff they comfort me. **AMEN**

Thought of the week
I will meet You in the darkness, even there

It had been an interesting year. I had been blessed with such amazing highs, where I had scaled mountains I never dreamed I would conquer. I'd basked in the rays of beauty and warmth and I'd found joy in the act of living I never knew possible.

But all of a sudden I found myself facing the darkness and the menacing tentacles of trouble and human frailty threatened to overwhelm me, as tiredness and drudgery formed dark pools around me. Yet, I have come to appreciate the darkness because I know that God is there, even when each step feels leadened and heavy. Even in the darkness I can find His tender mercies.

I didn't know why the valley stood before me, it didn't matter. My joy came from knowing that even there in the thick darkness, He was with me and even there where my eyes failed me, He would lead me. For the *"dark places"* are not dark to Him and He is fully able to see, even when I am not. *(See: Psalm 139:11-12).*

God inhabits the darkness

Psalm 18:11 *"He made darkness His secret place; His canopy around Him was dark waters and thick clouds of the skies."*

Psalm 97:2 *"Clouds and darkness surround Him; Righteousness and justice are the foundation of His throne"*

In Exodus 20:21, Moses drew near to the thick darkness. He chose to be where God was even when that place was frightening and uncomfortable. He chose to move beyond immense fear and human weakness in order to be in the place that God asked him to be. He drew near to the thick darkness and had a personal encounter with God and because of this was forever changed.

And what of the Israelites?

They had also been invited to meet with God on Mount Sinai, but fear for their mortal lives took root in their hearts and robbed them of a blessing far greater than life itself, the opportunity to encounter God first hand. Instead they watched from afar as another stepped up. They preferred to *'play it safe'* and live on the coat tails of Moses' experience than to risk all for the chance to meet with God personally.

1 John 1:5 says that *"...God is light and in Him is no darkness at all."* Yes, God is light but he is also Lord of the darkness, your darkness, my darkness and the darkness that encompasses the world.

Isaiah 45:7 *"I form the light and create darkness, I make peace and create calamity; I, the Lord, do all these things."*

I don't always understand why dark times come but I am learning to rest in them because I have come to know that my greatest opportunities for growth have come out of the darkest moments in my life. If being in the dark means remaining close to God then there I am content to stay, for however long on whatever path He deems I need to travel.

So often we view darkness as something to be feared and avoided but even in the darkness there is opportunity and treasure to be found. When we draw near to God in the darkness and have no way of creating our own light, He becomes our light and is able to lead us through situations and circumstances and teach us to trust in a way we never would have otherwise.

The enemy may rejoice when we appear to walk in the valley of darkness but he rejoices in vain because even in apparent darkness we have victory. For when we sit in darkness, the Lord becomes our light *(See Micah 7:8)* and He guides us onward and upward, all the while establishing our faith and strengthening our attachment to the vine.

Lessons from Mount Sinai

Defeated by abdication... The Israelites didn't want to approach God for fear that might lose something, in this case their lives. What they failed to recognise was the amount they stood to gain. Perhaps they would have died mortally (or to self) or perhaps they would have been radically transformed but they would never know, they abdicated their encounter into the hands of Moses and received a second hand experience as a result. How often do we do this? Out of fear or laziness we view God from a distance and abdicate our experience of God into the hands of someone else... The Pastor? The Worship Team? The Youth Leader? Someone wiser? Someone older? Someone more educated? Readily accepting what is fed to us on Sunday but never seeking His face or drawing near to Him for ourselves?

Lord, I will go because You asked me to

A nation was invited but only one encountered God first hand. A recount of the event in *Hebrews 12:21* says that Moses was *"exceedingly afraid and trembling"*. Moses had the same fears as the masses yet he moved beyond them because he loved the Lord his God and he wanted to be where He was. Are you willing, like Moses to move beyond your fear and trembling? Are you willing to be obedient to God's call even when it seems contrary to what is rational and in line with what everyone else is doing? Are you willing to stand as an example of courageous faith for the sake of others? When standing at the crossroads of decision, will you back away from God when faced with the thick darkness or draw near even if it might cost you your life as you know it?

"Let us therefore come boldly to the
throne of grace, that we may
obtain mercy and find grace to help in time of need."
Hebrews 4:16

WEEK 48

HIS TENDER MERCIES

Scripture of the week

Psalm 40:11 *"Do not withhold Your tender mercies from me, O Lord; let Your loving kindness and Your truth continually preserve me."*

Prayer of the week

Lord, when my soul is anguished I will praise You. Let me never forget that You are good and that Your mercy endures forever. For even when I fail, I am reminded that Your plans and purposes never change. Even when I miss the mark, I am reminded that You are steadfast and Your love never changes. In the midst of my human weaknesses, You are gracious Lord and full of compassion. I praise You Lord, I thank You for Your loving kindness. **AMEN**

Thought of the week

Quote:
"The revelation of God to each individual is made in form and manner tenderly agreeable to the condition and capacity of the favoured one."
(Charles Sturgeon)

Luke 1 :78-79 *"Through the tender mercy of our God, with which the Dayspring from on high has visited us; to give light to those who sit in darkness and the shadow of death, to guide our feet into the way of peace."*

Definition: 'Dayspring'... *dawn, dawning of the east, the rising of the sun, the beginning of a new era or order, the coming Messiah.*

Have you ever sat and watched the sunrise and found yourself holding your breath for fear that the very act of inhaling will somehow disturb the splendour of its dawning? Motionlessly transfixed, intent on absorbing the magnificence of the moment, enraptured in the beauty, not wanting to miss a single ray of light and feeling as if for just that moment in time God had sensed your need and orchestrated it just for you?

I love to watch the rising and the setting of the sun, to hear the waves crashing on the shore and water trickling over river beds. I am awed by how beautiful the dew is as it glistens on a newly formed spider web and I marvel at the elegance of a single leaf as it twists and spins, dancing effortlessly to the music of the wind. It is in these moments that I feel closest to God and I get a glimpse of His majesty and glory. It is in these moments that the truth of His goodness wedges firmly in my spirit and His tender mercies speak loudest to my heart.

I wonder, have you experienced a time where God has met you just where you are at? When you have sought His will in a situation and He has provided encouragement or confirmation at a time that you needed it most—a moment of recognition that spoke directly to your heart, bringing with it hope and renewed courage; a touch from his hand that caused your eyes to look upward and your heart to press forward or; a treasured moment of insight that provided assurance that He sees your situation and cares for you individually?

If you feel that God has overlooked you, I encourage you to spend some time in prayer asking Him to open your *spiritual* eyes to the tender mercies He is bestowing on your life. They are there, but sometimes we miss them or just don't recognise them because we are too busy or too consumed with the problem to watch expectantly for His answer.

Sometimes we just need to STOP and still our mind and our body long enough to hear His Spirit speaking or working in our lives.

From mud to music

King David understood the tender mercies of the Lord and was delivered out the depths of the miry clay. The words of **Psalm 40** say that he **"cried out to God"** (*spent time in prayer*) and **"God heard his prayer and inclined His ear"**. God not only set his feet on solid ground but in his *tender* mercy went beyond this and placed a 'new song' in his mouth.

Psalm 40:1-3 *"I waited patiently for the Lord; and He inclined to me, and heard my cry. He also brought me up out of a horrible pit, out of the miry clay, and set my feet upon a rock, and established my steps. He has put a new song in my mouth, praise to our God; many will see it and fear, and will trust in the Lord."* (A Psalm of David).

In my life, there have been some truly pinnacle moments that epitomise the tender mercies of God, many of which have come in the form of timely words of encouragement. Others have been instigated by something as simple as unexpected sunlight filtering through the windshield and warming my flesh when I have felt cold, tired and exhausted. It could be said that the sunlight was merely coincidence but as its rays broke forth from the clouds and warmed my skin my spirit connected with that of the Father and in that instant I recognised it as being His gift to me in that moment. His presence not only brought warmth to my body but renewed vigour and courage and a willingness to press on.

God is not only merciful to His children but is tenderly so. And, the greatest expression of His tender mercy is His '*Dayspring from on High*'. And so it is from the tender mercy of our God that He sent Jesus, the '*Dayspring from on High*' that we might not only be saved from the curse of sin but also enraptured and changed by His presence in our lives. For indeed, God knew our need and orchestrated Christ's coming that we might find redemption through His blood and perpetual delight in living and walking by His spirit.

> *Such is the overwhelming loveliness of*
> *His tender mercy towards us.*

WEEK 49

THE MASTER OF DISGUISE

Scripture of the week

I Peter 5:6-8 "*Therefore humble yourselves under the mighty hand of God, that He may exalt you in due time, casting all your care upon Him, for He cares for you. Be sober, be vigilant; because your adversary the devil walks about like a roaring lion, seeking whom he may devour.*"

Prayer of the week

Holy Spirit convict me, that I might lay down my anxiety, fear and cares in an attitude of humble confession and repentance, daily, hourly, constantly. That I might walk in freedom and emotional, physical and spiritual health, free from the chains of bondage that Jesus death and resurrection has set me free from. Quicken my spirit when I fail to let go of those things which will render me ineffective and threaten to hold me in bondage. Remind me that repentance and right relationship with You takes precedence over the constant demands of daily living, even when those things seem overwhelmingly important. Lord, I pray that I will always hear Your voice clearly, that I would urgently desire to maintain a pure and intimate relationship with You, for without You I am ineffectual. May my life be music to Your ears and a sweet fragrance to Your nose. In Jesus name. **AMEN**

Thought of the week
The master of disguise

Quote:
"Sunlight is the best disinfectant."
(William O. Douglas)

Ever since I was a child I have suffered from 'bad skin', a condition that became substantially worse after the birth of my children. My dad used to call me *'the bandaid bandit from Bandiwallop'* because I was constantly smothered in bandaids in a vain attempt to stop me from picking and scratching at it.

The doctors said it was an anxiety disorder that stemmed from habitually suppressing and ignoring how I was feeling and it is true that my skin is often at its worst when I am struggling to keep it all together. But as I am discovering more about who I am and my reactions to life, I am beginning to suspect that it is less an issue with anxiety and more an issue of trust or of *letting go and letting God.*

So over the years I have become an expert with a makeup brush and I can cover up the most insidious of marks with a bit of time and artistic ability but to what value. I cannot hide from God.

I am becoming increasingly convinced that healing and growth can only come when we are willing to be transparent, to be open and honest about our struggles,

243

to ourselves and each other, supporting one another in love and without judgement. Encouraging and exhorting one another and bringing our needs, individually and corporately to God in prayer, scars, warts and all.

James 5:16 *"Confess your trespasses to one another, and pray for one another, that you may be healed. The effective, fervent prayer of a righteous man avails much."*

God told me right from the first devotion that *'it starts with me'* and I am committed to being obedient to His leading. He has placed this issue of transparency and accountability among His people on my heart and I believe that we can only grow in spiritual maturity when we allow those things that we struggle with to be exposed to *'the light'*—God's light. *'Sonlight'* is truly the best disinfectant!

Malachi 4:2 *"But to you who fear My name, The Sun of Righteousness shall arise With healing in His wings; and you shall go out and grow fat like stall-fed calves."*

His yoke is not heavy

As I was journaling recently I found myself pouring my heart out to God about what He is trying to teach me in this battle with my skin and why at times when I feel most vulnerable it flares up and is at its worst. I have had prayer and I have prayed myself. I have bound and loosed and still it plagues me and the word that keeps coming to mind is 'trust'... *"Fee, do you trust me enough to let go and let Me? There is no shame in the struggle but you could save yourself a lot of heartache and anxiety if you would just learn to let go and rest completely in Me. My yoke is not heavy."*

Matthew 11:28-30 *"Come to Me, all you who labour and are heavy laden, and I will give you rest. Take My yoke upon you and learn from Me, for I am gentle and lowly in heart, and you will find rest for your souls. For My yoke is easy and My burden is light."*

The yoke of Jesus is light because when He died and rose again He released us from the bondage and burden of the law. But, when we do things in our own strength, in many ways we are placing ourselves again under self-imposed bondage that Jesus released us from. The yoke of Jesus is light because it is not a yoke of enslavement but a bond founded in a loving relationship with our gentle and caring Saviour, who willingly choose to shoulder the weight of our burdens. It is the yoke made available to us through repentance and faith and where our lives are no longer subject to a set of rules we *'dare not break'* but instead to heeding the voice of a faithful and trusted friend we long to walk in unity with.

So when I fail to maintain relationship, I also place myself in a position where is it harder to hear His voice and counsel clearly. Subsequently, I fail to hear and move within the wisdom of His leading and I fall into the trap of trying to struggle on alone, pushing through in my own strength and making choices based on my own wisdom. Jesus was in constant communion with His Father. He brought His concerns and fears to God and found solace and rest in His counsel. Indeed we would save ourselves much anguish and anxiety if we would only learn from and follow His example.

So, by internalising and 'bottling up' rather than confessing my fears and failures and negative emotions as they arise, I place a yoke of bondage on myself that He never intended for me to shoulder.

A friend mentioned that she was reading a book and they described it something like this... (not the exact words but the general gist) *Christ has set us free, the chains are broken, but for some reason we insist on picking them up and carrying them around with us.*

So my question is... do you rattle as you walk?

Are you prone, like me, to picking up and stumbling under the weight of the chains of bondage instead of leaving them at the cross where Jesus broke their power and rendered us free?

This is not your portion. This is not my portion. The Lord is our portion and He maintains our lot!

Psalm 16:5-11 *"O Lord, You are the portion of my inheritance and my cup; You maintain my lot. The lines have fallen to me in pleasant places; yes, I have a good inheritance. I will bless the Lord who has given me counsel; my heart also* *instructs me in the night seasons. I have set the Lord always before me; because He is at my right hand I shall not be moved. Therefore my heart is glad, and my glory rejoices; my flesh also will rest in hope. For You will not leave my soul in Sheol, nor will You allow Your Holy One to see corruption. You will show me the path of life; in Your presence is fullness of joy; at Your right hand are pleasures forevermore."*

WEEK 50

REFINER'S FIRE

Scripture of the week

Proverbs 25:4 *"Take away the dross from silver, and it will go to the silversmith for jewellery"* (some versions say it can be used to make a vessel).

Prayer of the week

Turn up the heat O Lord, make me an instrument of pure 'mettle', forged in Your furnace, *even the furnace of affliction*. Make me usable Lord, purposefully remove the dross from my life to reveal a pure and precious metal that is suitable for crafting into a vessel of Your choosing. Establish my character by Your refining fire so that one day You might look upon me and see Your face reflected in my substance. Stay near and watch over me Lord. Uphold me by Your righteous hand for in You I trust. I will not be dismayed. For You are my strength and my salvation. **AMEN**

Thought of the week
Dross

Definition: *Something that is worthless or of low standard or quality. Also defined as the scum formed on molten metals.*

There is a story by an unknown author which speaks of a woman who asked a silversmith if she could watch him undertake the process of refining silver. Now, I am not sure how much 'technical' credence can be attributed to this tale but it is a powerful analogy of God's refining influence in our lives, so this is my 'subtitled' paraphrase of the story.

STEP 1: Turn up the heat to remove the dross
As the woman watched the silversmith, he explained that the silver had to be positioned and held in the middle of the flames where it was hottest so that the impurities would be burned away and the dross then removed to leave the pure metal.

STEP 2: Carefully watch and remove from the heat at just the right moment
Malachi 3:3 "And He shall sit as a refiner and purifier of silver."

She then asked the silversmith why it was necessary for him to sit and watch the silver as it went through the process of removing the dross and he replied that he not only had to sit there but he had to keep his eyes on the silver the entire time it was in the fire, for if the silver was subjected to the heat a moment too long, it would be destroyed.

STEP 3: The moment of truth, treasure revealed
She pondered for a while and then enquired of the silversmith once more, 'So, how do you know when the silver is fully

*refined?' He smiled at her and answered, '**Oh, that's easy—
when I can see my image in it**.'*

So, in the process of refining silver heat is applied to the
raw material in order to destroy and remove the impurities
leaving only the pure and usable metal behind.

Isaiah 48:10 *"Behold, I have refined you, but not as silver;
I have tested you in the furnace of affliction..."*

The Bible tells us that the spiritual furnace that God
chooses to refine us is the ***furnace of affliction***. Spiritual
refinement is the process through which we become
Christ-like, a process through which the dross and residue
of our 'old man' is destroyed and removed leaving only the
truth and purity of Christ in us. This story shows God's
perfect purpose and timing in each of our lives as He uses
the 'heat' and trials of our lives to strip away that which
is worthless, leaving us only with that which is pure,
undefiled and usable. Each moment spent in the refiner's
fire brings us one step closer to that place where our very
substance becomes a mirror image and reflection of Jesus.

God never promised that we would travel through
life without trials and tribulations but He did say that
He would be with us and uphold us and He *IS* there
overseeing the refining process of our lives, watching and
removing us from the heat in His perfect timing so that in
undergoing the process of perfecting, we are not destroyed
but made usable.

Isaiah 41:10 *"Fear not, for I am with you; Be not dismayed, for I am your God. I will strengthen you, Yes, I will help you, I will uphold you with My righteous right hand."*

With such incredible skill, wisdom and insight God removes the dross from our lives, simultaneously purifying the precious metal beneath. In the process of refining the value and usability of the metal *(you)* is revealed. Often it is only in the purification process that we become aware of the precious metal within and whilst God always knew it existed, we can be surprised at what was once hidden beneath the layers of scum that once defined us.

Many seeds never flourish or produce fruit until they have been exposed to heat of a bushfire and often it is the circumstances in our lives that reveal qualities in our lives that would never have been revealed otherwise.

Sometimes God asks us to step into the fire fully armed with the knowledge that the process He is asking us to undertake is ultimately for our benefit and will produce perseverance and character that will allow us to successfully navigate the road He has asked us to travel. Other times He may simply ask that we endure the afflictions that come our way as He uses them to prepare us for a purpose we may not yet know.

The fire incinerates the lies you believe about yourself, it tests your faith, your resolve and your convictions and when you have endured the flames and allowed God to re-shape your thinking and your very substance, you discover qualities—good qualities, that you never knew were in you. Suffering is God's instrument to bring about growth in our lives.

Will you stand in the furnace of affliction and allow God, the 'master refiner' to purge you from the dross of your life? Will you patiently endure the heat knowing that God will use it to purify and create endurance in your faith and Christ-like qualities in your Christian walk?

For those seeking purpose in your life; are you willing to be refined so that the Lord can create from you a usable vessel? Often we ask for purpose and direction but are we willing to undergo the process God requests of us in order for Him to make us usable?

> *"My brethren, count it all joy when*
> *you fall into various trials,*
> *knowing that the testing of your faith produces patience.*
> *But let patience have its perfect work, that you*
> *may be perfect and complete, lacking nothing.*
> ***James 1:2-4***

WEEK 51

CULTURALLY CHALLENGED

Scripture of the week

Revelation 7:9 *"After these things I looked, and behold, a great multitude which no one could number, of all nations, tribes, peoples, and tongues, standing before the throne and before the Lamb, clothed with white robes, with palm branches in their hands."*

Prayer of the week

Lord, make me an instrument of Your peace that I would seek to tear down the barriers that stand between myself and those You have asked me to serve. That I would seek to understand their 'reality' even if that means moving beyond the comfort of my own. Let me see others through Heaven's eyes and show them practical love just as You would have. Convict me if I become complacent in my faith and stir me to action when I am in danger of becoming nothing but a clanging cymbal. In Jesus name. **AMEN**

Thought of the week
Culturally challenged

I recently attended 'preview week' at a College that I was considering applying to study at. My aim was to 'check it out' and try and get confirmation that this is where God wanted me enrol. The college has a 'missional' focus and their primary aim is to 'fully' prepare those called to cross cultural missions. As well as teaching it also has a large focus on 'community' and personal and spiritual development. It is not just about getting the bit of paper at the end, but immersing yourself in a way of living that also prepares you psychologically and spiritually for the challenges that will inevitably be thrust at you once you enter the field. I was there for only one week but challenged I was, and not for the reasons I thought.

I am by nature a human *'doer'* and so the practical aspects of community I was pretty much able to take in my stride. Give me a task and I will run with it. I am not afraid to get my hands dirty and will generally be able to competently achieve whatever task is asked of me, that's what *'doers'* do. I am definitely *'task'* orientated—no challenge there.

I took an educated guess that I would struggle when it came to the 'relational' stuff, right again! My inclination was to hide in my dorm when I wasn't *'tasking something'* and it took every bit of my resolve to force myself out the door and mingle in the communal areas or make small talk with staff and students but I managed to push past myself and I guess I will get better at this over time and with practice.

The element however that took me by surprise was my reaction to being surrounded by people from unfamiliar cultures and as I have reflected on this in an effort to understand my reaction I have realised that I am very 'culturally challenged' and severely lacking in my understanding of cultures other than my own. I also realise that I am possibly in greater danger of *'self shock'* than *'culture shock'* as I step out into cross-cultural missions.

I grew up in an *'Anglo'* family, with *'Anglo'* friends who all attended *'Anglo'* schools. The majority of my working life has been spent surrounded by *'Anglo'* co-workers and I have always attended churches with a fairly high *'Anglo'* membership. I pretty much know how to operate and communicate within the context of my low-middle class *'Anglo'* comfort zone.

Now this is not to say that I have not had contact with people whose origins are different to my own but it has been minimal and generally only for short periods from which I then re-enter the familiarity of *'my own'* cultural territory. At the college, *'Anglo'* Australians were in the minority and 'living' (even for this short time) out of my 'cultural comfort zone' consumed huge amounts of energy and challenged me immensely. I did not understand their culture and for the most part they did not understand me and I was shocked by my negative reaction and irrational desire to avoid contact with other people at all costs. It was more than just a barrier of language, although this aspect did play a major part in being able to decode and break down the invisible walls that seemed to stand between us.

In this environment, I never really knew what was appropriate in terms of behaviour and verbal responses or whether the next thing I did or said was going to offend someone. I even struggled to understand what was expected of me as female. In the context of this multi-cultural community I seemed to be 'loud' and 'forward' and 'overly confident' even when I was trying to be reserved. I found that I was constantly on alert just in case in the very act of being myself, I inadvertently offended someone and for the most part nobody got my sense of humour. Who I am didn't fit naturally or cleanly and it was very disconcerting.

What was also interesting was to observe the other students as they a) mix with students from their own culture and b) mix with students from other cultures, they are animated and free when engaging with students from their own culture but 'less free' when interacting with students whose country of origin is different to their own. Perhaps I wasn't the only fish out of water.

During this week I was frequently surrounded by people but felt very alone. I felt very out of my comfort zone and I laughed silently as His words kept ringing in my ears, *"I don't want you to be comfortable"*. I got the sense that I was experiencing a small 'taste' of the very thing I now know in my heart God wants to deal with on a larger scale. He is asking me if I am willing to step into the fire and be refined in this area.

Interestingly, as I made an effort to move beyond my awkwardness and listen to peoples stories in often very 'broken English', I have come to realise that what I think I 'know' is actually very little and that there is much to be learned from living in community and rubbing shoulders with others (regardless of culture), lessons that do not involve text books and lectures and; I am beginning to realise that it is impossible to truly love from 'afar' and that loving effectively means being willing to become involved in the lives of others in the context of *their* reality. When we choose to move out of our comfort zones in order to try and understand another's reality then we take giant steps in breaking down the cultural misunderstandings that separate us from each other.

Culture, a matter of perspective

Definition of Culture: *The ideas, customs, and social behaviour of a particular people or society* (Oxford Dictionary Online)

My experience at preview week focused very much on culture according to nationality but in truth, the definition of 'culture' is much broader than just country of origin. There are cultures and sub-cultures within nationalities, groups, sexes, ages and interest groups. There is a culture of people who scrapbook (I am not one of them) but those who are know the terms, the lingo, the mode of operation and the social etiquette that encompasses the 'culture' of scrapbooking. I would probably feel just as out of place in this culture as I did at Bible college—well maybe not quite but you get the idea.

To take this train of thought one step further, I have noticed that churches also tend to operate within an implicit 'culture' brought about by the people who attend the church. People look for a place to 'fit' when looking for a church and if they find it, they generally stay and if they don't, they move on. Humans like to find a place to feel comfortable and which best accommodates our own way of looking at the world, a place that does not challenge their thinking or status quo too much. Unconsciously, we embrace those who are like us and avoid those who are not.

Waking up from our cultural coma

1 Corinthians 13:1 "*Though I speak with the tongues of men and of angels, but have not love, I have become sounding brass or a clanging cymbal.*"

But what happens when someone or something upsets our apple cart and behaves or says something that does not quite fit what is culturally acceptable to the mindset of the majority? What is our response? Do we shut them out or do we make an effort to understand their reality? I guess we need to ask ourselves, what would Jesus have done? If we truly take the higher road and temper our words and actions with love, we may in the process find ourselves treading unfamiliar ground and way out of our comfort zone. *Praise the Lord!* He does not want us to be comfortable, because when we get comfortable we are in danger of becoming nothing more than religious pew warmers and clanging cymbals.

Whilst never compromising His faith or watering down the truth of the gospel, Paul stood as an example to us as we deal with those from different cultures and 'worldviews'. He took the time to understand the perspective of those who were different to himself, the Jew, the non-Jew and the weak. Wherever possible he sought to actively embrace and understand the culture of the people he ministered to in order to 'meet them where they were at', to love them and to bring them to a place in which they might receive salvation.

1 Corinthians 9:19-23 *"For though I am free from all men, I have made myself a servant to all, that I might win the more; and to the Jews I became as a Jew, that I might win Jews; to those who are under the law, as under the law, that I might win those who are under the law; to those who are without law, as without law (not being without law toward God, but under law toward Christ, that I might win those who are without law; to the weak I became as weak, that I might win the weak. I have become all things to all men, that I might by all means save some. Now this I do for the gospel's sake, that I may be partaker of it with you."*

Rejecting the status quo

Is there someone in your church or in your life that you just can't relate to? Do they push your buttons or make you feel uncomfortable in some way-*too loud; too quiet; too quirky or; too different*? Do you pretend to look the other way to avoid making eye contact that might result in having to acknowledge them in conversation? I have to admit that I have been guilty of this for no other reason that I just didn't want to move beyond my comfort zone, instead seeking out a familiar face and heading directly for them.

But, perhaps they too are feeling out of their depth; perhaps they also do not know how to break through the barriers that create a distance between you; perhaps by finding a way to connect with that person, you provide them with an expression of love and acceptance that spurs them on in their walk. *'In Heaven's eyes there are no losers'...* may our perspective be Heavenly.

> *"...but glory, honour, and peace to*
> *everyone who works what is good,*
> *to the Jew first and also to the Greek. For*
> *there is no partiality with God."*
> **Romans: 2:10-11**

WEEK 52

BIBLE STUDY WORKSHOP

A 10 Step Framework for Studying the Bible
Step 1: Decide on a Theme or Topic

Your theme may be inspired from:
- Something you have read
- A statement you have heard
- Something that is happening in your life

Step 2: Ask a question that you desire to be answered

Try and keep it short and a single sentence. Your question might start:
- How did..?
- Why did..?
- What did..?
- Who did..?
- When did..?
- Where did..?

Step 3: Identify the key word(s) in your question

These will form the basis of your study so only pick one or two important ones.
- Underline the words you have identified
  e.g. *"Does God <u>hear</u> me when I <u>cry</u>?"*

Step 4: Find synonyms for your keywords

A synonym is a word that has a similar meaning to the word you have chosen. Resources you could use:
- Thesaurus
- Online Thesaurus or internet search

Pick one or two that you think might you might find in the Bible.

Step 5: Define each key word /synonym

Try and get both an every-day definition and a Biblical definition if one is available. Resources you could use:
- Standard dictionary
- A Bible dictionary
- An online dictionary
- A Bible study website such as:
    o www.biblegateway.com
    o www.biblehub.com
    o www.studylight.org

- Bible Apps
    o Touch Bible
    o My Sword

Step 6: Find and Sort the scriptures

Using a concordance or online concordance search and locate all scriptures that contain the 'key' words or 'synonyms' you have listed above. The idea at this point is not to read all the scriptures in depth (as there is likely to be hundreds) but to *scan over the lists'* and write down those that appear relevant at first 'glance'. As you scan ask yourself, *"Does the scripture appear to be relevant to my question?"*

- Yes? Note the reference down
- No? Leave it off the list for the time being

Once you have completed the preliminary list. Read each scripture in context and cross out any that on further investigation are not really relevant to the topic.

Step 7: Analyse the remaining verses

Important: When analysing the verse make sure you read the verse in the <u>context</u> of the whole passage. It is very dangerous to extract 'bits' of verses or single verses and use them out of context. A verse on its own can be misinterpreted when taken out of the context of the situation in which it was written.

For each verse note any or all of the following insights or observations as relevant:
- Who is speaking?
- Who are they speaking to?
- What does the verse say in relation to my question?
- Is there a 'condition' attached to the verse eg. *If* you... *then* I will
- Any other observations or comments.

If you don't understand a verse, make a note to research it further using Commentaries, Bible Handbooks, Teachers in the Church and (as a last resort) Website Searches (sermons, podcasts etc).

Important: Be very careful when researching on the internet. There are a lot of good sites out there but there are also a lot of sites with some pretty 'weird' thinking. Reading sermons and other material online is good for expanding your thinking and giving you ideas on how to search further but TREAD CAREFULLY and don't just accept everything you read. A good sermon will back their claims with a solid scriptural foundation and they will not take verses out of context to suit their own purposes. Try and find websites that are transparent in their statement of faith and not 'fly by the nighters'. Ask the Holy Spirit to alert you when something is spiritually unsound.

Step 8: Draw conclusions

Look at the notes you have made against the verses you have studied:

- Is there a common theme?
- Have the verses answered your question?
- What is Gods view on the topic? (The Biblical perspective)
- How do these verses relate to you as a believer?
- What can I learn from this study?

Step 9: Life application

How can you apply what you have learnt in your daily walk?

- Is there an 'action' you need to take?

- Is there an 'attitude' you need to change?
- Is there a 'lie' you need to reject?
- Is there a 'promise' you need to embrace?

Step 10: Pray the scriptures

How can we know we are praying in the will of God? One of the best ways is to pray the scriptures. Using the scriptures from the study create a prayer that you can pray over your life and the lives of others.

For example:
Therefore I remind you to *stir up the gift of God which is in you* through the laying on of my hands. *For God has not given us a spirit of fear, but of power and of love and of a sound mind.*" *2 Timothy 1:6-7*

In these verses, the Apostle Paul is encouraging Timothy (who is a bit on the shy side) to stir up the gifts that were in him and which were made known to him through the laying on of hands (being prayed for). He goes on to pretty much say that you are capable of doing this not in your own strength but because you have the Spirit of God, and His spirit is not subject to fear, but power and love and a sound mind.

So... praying 2 Timothy 1:6-7 might look something like this:

Lord, I thank You for *the gifts that You have placed within me*. I pray that You would make these gifts clear to me and show me how I can use them for Your glory. As a child of Your kingdom I am empowered by Your Holy Spirit. *I do not have a spirit of fear* but of *love and of power and of a sound mind*. Give me the courage to step out in faith and use that which You have given me. **AMEN**

About the Author

Capable, emotionally insecure, fiercely independent... *Oh wait! That's not me!* That women is dead and buried! Praise God! Let me start again! Empowered by *His* Spirit, sustained by *His* grace and fiercely dependent on *Him*. My life is a living testament to His grace and from the 'Valley of Achor' He showed me the door of hope.

Postscript

Felicity has a heart to see women thrive spiritually, even in the face of seemingly insurmountable adversity. It is her desire to bring a message of hope and salvation to women who through no fault of their own and often as a result of war, abuse and poverty, are struggling just to survive each day.

The proceeds of this book will initially be used to help fund her studies as she undertakes full-time Theological training. At the completion of her qualification she will partner with her home and local churches who, in conjunction with an International Mission Organisation, will collaboratively form her support team as she enters the mission field full-time.

Your support in this work is greatly appreciated and may God bless you abundantly as you partner with Felicity through the sale of her book.

For further information, please contact Felicity via her Facebook page at https://www.facebook.com/profile.php?id=100006576376305.